A beginner's Guide to

CROSSING
Cultures

making

friends

in a

multi-

cultural

world

Patty Lane

InterVarsity Press
Downers Grove, Illinois

InterVarsity Press
P.O. Box 1400, Downers Grove, IL 60515-1426
World Wide Web: www.ivpress.com
E-mail: mail@ivpress.com

InterVarsity Press® is the book-publishing division of InterVarsity Christian Fellowship/U.S.A®,
a student movement active on campus at hundreds of universities, colleges and schools of
nursing in the United States of America, and a member movement of the International
Fellowship of Evangelical Students. For information about local and regional activities, write
Public Relations Dept., InterVarsity Christian Fellowship/U.S.A, 6400 Schroeder Rd., P.O. Box
7895, Madison, WI 53707-7895, or visit the IVCF website at <www.ivcf.org>.

All Scripture quotations, unless otherwise indicated, are taken from the Holy Bible, New
International Version®. NIV®. Copyright ©1973, 1978, 1984 by the International Bible Society.
Used by permission of Zondervan Publishing House. All rights reserved.

Cover design: Design Concepts

Cover photography: © Photodisc

ISBN 0-8308-2346-8

Printed in the United States of America ∞

Library of Congress Cataloging-in-Publication Data

Lane, Patty.
  A beginner's guide to crossing cultures: making friends in a multicultural world/Patty Lane.
    p. cm.
  Includes bibliographical references.
  ISBN 0-8308-2346-8 (pbk.: alk. paper)
    1. Cross-cultural orientation. 2. Intercultural communication. 3. Multiculturalism. I.
  Title.
  GN345.65 .L26 2002
  303.48'2—dc21   2002019713

P	17	16	15	14	13	12	11	10	9	8	7	6	5	4	3	2	1
Y	15	14	13	12	11	10	09	08	07	06	05	04	03	02			

Contents

Acknowledgments

No project like this is ever undertaken alone or completed without the help of many friends and coworkers. I have been blessed with faithful companions on this journey without whom there would be no book. Their encouragement and support mean so much to me. There are too many to call by name, so I will only mention a few.

I am very grateful to Karen Simons, who challenged me to begin writing this book—a task I would have otherwise never attempted. Others along the way, Bill Pinson and Joy Fenner specifically, never let me forget I also needed to finish.

Several assisted in the editing of the manuscript: Martha King, Janice Byrd and Cathy Butler. They were both patient and challenging as they spent hours correcting and clarifying my written words. Jeannie Bordovsky walked me through many a computer scare with the calmness needed to keep me going and keep me sane.

But without the hundreds of pastors and church members I have had the privilege of working with, I would have nothing to write about. It is because they have so graciously shared their lives with me—their joys, their hurts, their frustrations, their relationship with God—that I have been blessed beyond measure. They have shaped my life in countless ways, and I will always be in their debt.

Introduction

As humans we have a great deal in common with each other. We all need to eat, to sleep, to love and be loved. Yet our commonalities are sometimes hard to see, because from the time of our birth we are cultural beings. A simple definition of culture is "a system of meanings and values that shape one's behavior."[1] Geert Hofstede, a noted cultural researcher, defines culture as "the collective programming of the mind which distinguishes the members of one human group from another."[2]

Our culture shapes who we are, what we believe and how we behave. At no point in our human interactions do we take off our culture and set it aside. It is always with us in all of our relationships, in all of our thinking and our processing of the world around us.

Our world is changing rapidly, calling for new skills and knowledge in order for us to survive and prosper. Because of the interactions between nations and ethnic groups, our skills in forming and maintaining relationships with those who are culturally different from us will be critical for our success in the new millennium.

This book is a skill-building journey into crosscultural relationships—working with persons of more than one cultural background—learning the connections we must make in order for our interactions to be healthy and meaningful. The approach is simple: connecting our heads (cognitive process), hearts (emotional process) and hands (application process) in each chapter. This is not a new process for learning, but rather one that dates back to the earliest of recorded history. In this regard, Deuteronomy 6 is a pivotal passage for both Jews and Christians. The fourth verse, the Shema, states "Hear, O Israel: The LORD our God is one LORD; and you shall love the LORD your God with all your heart, and with all your soul, and with all your might" (RSV).

From the beginning God knew we needed to connect what we know with what we feel and what we do. Piaget and others in the field of educational psychology have explained the benefit of connecting these three elements in order for true learning to take place.[3] While their research was within a European and U.S. American context, I believe the principle is universal and appropriate for all cultures.[4]

This book's perspective is quite specific. Most books written on crosscultural understanding and communication focus on the U.S. American living abroad or the international residing temporarily in the United States. This book, however, looks specifically at the peculiarities of the United States' multicultural environment (U.S. born and foreign born) and will be a useful tool for persons of any culture who find themselves in a relationship with someone of another culture.

The purpose is practical. The discipline of cultural anthropology guides and informs our study, but the focus is on the application of that discipline to crosscultural relationships. At the end of each chapter you will find specific exercises to reinforce the application. The appendices include materials for further individual and group learning. The emphasis is on connecting knowledge with feelings and using this connection to make a difference in your life and in the world.

The questions that will be answered in this book reflect the basic struggles confronting individuals who function within a multicultural environment.

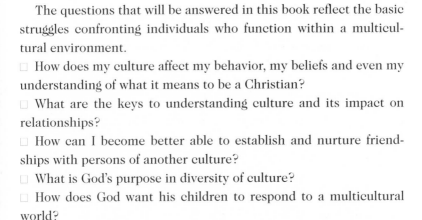

☐ How does my culture affect my behavior, my beliefs and even my understanding of what it means to be a Christian?

☐ What are the keys to understanding culture and its impact on relationships?

☐ How can I become better able to establish and nurture friendships with persons of another culture?

☐ What is God's purpose in diversity of culture?

☐ How does God want his children to respond to a multicultural world?

As your assumptions are challenged, your own questions, unique to you and your context, will surface. This is a good thing and can be the catalyst to seeking new relationships and resources that will provide the additional answers you need.

This book's context is Christian. Biblical principles are woven into the cultural insights, informing and motivating new attitudes and actions. In the past many Christians have been silent regarding social issues confronting society, such as slavery and integration. We stand at another social crossroads created by our country's rapidly changing demographics. Who would be better than the Christian community to lead society in the development of successful, healthy crosscultural relationships?

Several years ago I was leading a conference at the annual international meeting of SIETAR (Society for Intercultural Education, Training and Research) in Washington, D.C. As part of my presentation on crosscultural conflict resolution, i explained that while I had years of experience dealing with conflicts between culture groups, I had not had formal training in this area. A young man came up to speak with me afterwards. He commented, "Your conference was very helpful and unique. I am a graduate student in intercultural studies and I have never heard anyone give such practical and helpful information. I know you said you did not have formal training, but you must be reading someone. Who and what have you been studying?"

I appreciated his compliment, but had never thought about what I was reading or whom I was studying. I just blurted out, "The Bible and the life of Jesus." I wondered how this intellectual young man would react. He looked amazed and stood there in silence as others came by to talk and ask questions. Soon he was the only one left. As he walked away, he said softly, "Well, you have given me a reason to read one [a Bible]."

I have never spoken to him again, but the incident both changed and challenged me. People throughout the world are searching for successful ways to live and work together. As Christians, we have the solution. When we make the connections between our heads, our hearts and our hands, we will be able to create healthy environments for multicultural relationships and reflect the light of Jesus in our world.

Note. The illustrations used have had the names changed to protect confidentiality, and on some occasions, represent a composite of situations.

The term "U.S. American" is used instead of "American" because it is limited to those in the United States and does not include North and Central America.

The dominant culture refers to the culture having the most influence in a specific area, not the largest population group.

1

What Is Our
Cultural Landscape?

Did You Know?

☐ *Los Angeles is now the second largest Iranian city in the world.*

☐ *Chicago has more Poles than San Francisco has people.*

☐ *One-third of the world's Jews live in the United States.*

☐ *In the United States there are more Buddhists than Episcopalians.*

☐ *In California, 239 languages are spoken; in New York, 184; in Washington, 181; in Texas, 169.*

☐ *More than 400,000 international students from 181 countries study at American universities.*[1]

When I was in elementary school, I learned that the United States was a "melting pot." I pictured in my mind what happened when I melted chocolate chips, butter and sweetened condensed milk together. When the melting was finished, the pretty yellow butter and the white milk were nowhere to be seen. Their sacrifice could be tasted, but all that was visible was the dark brown of the dominant ingredient—the chocolate. As a fourth grader, being a melting pot seemed like a good idea. I thought I was the chocolate and the ones who were different from me would be the ones to sacrifice for my benefit.

Later I learned that just within miles of the publishers of my fourth grade history book (the ones who extolled the virtues of the "melting pot") were whole communities that were Polish and Irish. There was a "little Italy" and a "Chinatown." The melting pot had not happened. As one looks around today, it is clear to see that it is still not a reality. New immigrants do not suddenly melt into the dominant U.S. culture simply by living in the United States.

Volumes have been written that trace and analyze the sociopolitical movements of our country, giving understanding to the multicultural environment we live in today. Books like *Border People— Life and Society in the U.S.-Mexico Borderlands* by Oscar J. Martinez deal even more specifically with unique areas of our country where two distinct cultures interact intensely and form their own cultural phenomenon. The United States is unique in its history, having been founded by immigrants who continue to arrive and contribute to the dominant culture. Similes abound for what U.S. society is like: a mosaic, a salad bowl or a quilt. All of these similes, while demonstrating how different items bring about a wonderful whole greater than all its parts, leave out an important element of what happens. Think about stew. In a stew pot the potatoes look like potatoes and taste like potatoes, but with the added savor of carrots, onions and beef. Each ingredient takes on some of the flavor of the other ingredients, without becoming invisible. Thus, the entire dish is more delicious and each ingredient is enhanced.

The United States is like stew. The individual cultures are recognizable, yet they influence each other and the flavors mix together. It is easy to see in this image the advantage of stew over soup that has been pureed into a uniform consistency. As connoisseurs of food we know which has the most appeal. Yet when it comes to culture many times we seem to want the pureed version, even though we will lose the rich textures, colors and unique flavors. This desire for conformity to the dominant culture marginalizes people and causes resentment toward cultures that resist being blended into the whole.

What Is Culture?
There are probably as many definitions of culture as there are recipes for stew. A simple one is "a system of meanings and values that shape one's behavior."[2] Everyone has a culture, but recognizing the

impact of culture on relationships is not always so easy.

Consider a classroom situation that has students who are from several cultures, but predominantly African American. As the teacher is lecturing about history, several African American students speak out with comments like, "That's right" and "You know it." This distracts the other students, some finding it an interruption and others considering it proof that African Americans have no consideration for others. Based on this, many decide that they do not want to be friends with the African American students. The teacher believes that racism is the cause of this obvious segregation. However, when students are interviewed about their relationships with their fellow classmates it is discovered that race is not the issue; it is the specific behaviors that have kept the students apart.

What a difference it would have made if the students had understood the African American traditions in church and in community life. Then they would have known that talking back to a speaker was both common practice and a sign of the audience's participation in the lecture. The African American students were not being rude—they were being themselves and actually complimenting the teacher by showing agreement. Because the cultures involved gave different meanings to the behavior, assumptions were made that caused relationships to be strained. Repeat this scenario over and over, thousands of times a day, and you have a glimpse of what we are facing in building relationships with persons of other cultures within the United States. Racism is real and it is destructive and wrong, but one place to begin to eliminate it is to begin to understand cultural differences.

Pick up the daily newspaper. How many stories do you see that involve other cultures in your city, state or nation? No matter the size of your local newspaper, you probably found at least one. You may have noticed an article about new immigrants or second generation Hispanics. You recognized that culture might be a factor in the story because the story identified a racial or ethnic background.

Or differences in appearance or language alerted you to the fact that there might be a cultural difference. At other times, however, the difference is not so easily seen.

For newcomers to the United States there is a pattern to the process of becoming a part of our cultural stew. Many different types of people arrive in the United States each day: immigrants, refugees, international students, undocumented people and businesspersons.[3] While each category of newcomer has special considerations and status within the Immigration and Naturalization Service (INS), for the moment we will consider them all the same.

Objective and Subjective Culture

Once a newcomer is here, some changes become noticeable almost immediately. A person's clothing, manner of greeting, diet and language may adapt to approximate the dominant culture where the person now lives. Those changes take place in what is referred to as their objective culture. Think about it like an iceberg. The visible part of culture is the objective part. It is the most easily recognized and the most easily changed. It is supported by the subjective culture—the part of the iceberg that is below the surface of the water. This is the

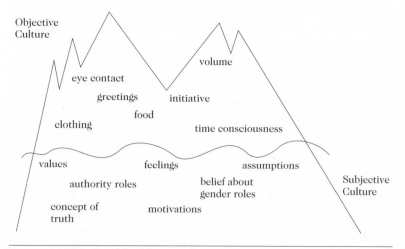

Figure 1.1. Objective and subjective culture

internal part of culture that drives or motivates the visible, objective culture. It consists of motivations, beliefs and worldview.[4]

Would you rather pilot a ship through an ocean full of icebergs where the tops are still visible or where someone has cut them off at sea level? The answer is obvious, yet many times we navigate in an ocean of people who are culturally different, but we do not recognize those differences. This is because the visible part of their culture has become less noticeable due to changes they have made to more closely reflect the culture of their new location. This is not only true of newcomers to the United States, but is true of culture groups who have been within our borders for multiple generations. Notice what happens in the following story.

In 1984 at the age of eighteen, Ha Nguyen arrived in the United States through a refugee resettlement program. He was sent to Houston, Texas, where he had relatives and where there was a strong Vietnamese community. The adjustment was difficult and learning English became his highest priority. He began working at a Vietnamese restaurant to earn some money. Soon he was able to serve the English-speaking customers. He was excited to know that his English was improving and that it would not be long before he would be able to attend the local community college.

On his first day of class he decided to tell his professors and classmates that his name was John instead of Ha. He had learned that in English Ha was not a name but a laugh. He did not want people to laugh at him. He also decided to buy sandwiches in the student center for lunch instead of taking the rice and spring rolls his aunt offered. Over the course of the next few months his clothing, speech, diet and mannerisms all began to look like those of the U.S.-born students at his college. One day his professor mentioned how remarkable it was that "John" had become American so quickly. What did his professor mean?

In the eyes of the professor, Ha was American in his objective culture and the assumption was that he had also changed his values and beliefs. In Ha's eyes, he saw that he was behaving more like his U.S. counterparts, but he still knew that much of what his new friends thought and valued, he found strange. He also recognized that when he talked about his family and their role in his decisions, his U.S. American friends did not understand. Ha's subjective culture had not changed. He was looking and talking more like an American, but his heart-language and culture were still Vietnamese.

The degree and speed of change of one's objective culture are determined by several factors. Which of these impacted Ha?

Age. The younger a person is when arriving in the United States, the quicker the person adapts their objective culture, and ultimately, their subjective culture.

Community. The community in which a newcomer resides influences the amount of visible changes the person makes. If the community has a large population from the immigrant's homeland, it will be easier to remain in that community and have most, if not all, one's needs met without mixing with the dominant U.S. culture. This will slow the adaptation of objective culture. If there are few or none from the country of origin, out of necessity adaptation will be faster.

Religion/faith. With most faith communities, beliefs and teachings are very closely linked to cultural values and behaviors. For religious adherents, changing their culture, even their objective culture, is extremely difficult. However, if a person experiences a change of faith after coming to the United States, it is more likely that aspects of culture will undergo some transformation. For instance, if a Christian becomes a Muslim, styles of clothing and greeting may change. Over time some aspects of subjective culture, such as worldview, will also be transformed, but will probably never be the same as a Middle Eastern counterpart. If a Buddhist becomes a Christian, objective culture will be modified to match those of the new faith community, while some U.S. values closely linked to Christianity may never be truly accepted.

Education. It appears that the more U.S. education the newcomer has, the more quickly objective culture will be modified. For students there is more exposure to U.S. culture and a strong desire to be accepted.

Employment. Employment opportunities for newcomers vary greatly depending on skills, contacts and visa status (permission granted by the Immigration and Naturalization Service to be in the United States). The more the exposure to the U.S. culture through employment, the more the objective culture will adapt. For example, if a Romanian immigrant works in a Romanian auto repair shop only with other Romanians and has little contact with U.S. American customers, adaptation of objective culture will be slower than if that same person worked at a Sears auto shop dealing with a variety of employees and customers.

English proficiency. The greater the level of English language skill, the more accommodation there is to the host or new culture. The adage that "you can't really know another culture until you know the language" is based on the truth that language holds keys to knowing cultural values and perspectives. "Language learning is the key to unlocking the secret code to another culture."[5]

The mere learning of English can teach values held by native English speakers. Syntax, grammar and idioms are all clues to the culture. For example, the Asian idiom "the poppy that grows higher than the others must be cut off" gives insight into the value of unity and uniformity. The pronoun "I" is always capitalized in English, but not so in other languages. Could this reflect the importance of the individual in English-speaking cultures? Understanding that in Arabic-speaking cultures the father takes on the name of the first son, making his name after the birth of the son "Abbu Riyad—father of Riyad"—indicates the importance of the oldest son within the culture.

Reason for coming to the United States. If a person has chosen to come to the U.S., there is greater motivation for changing some behaviors in order to become more easily accepted in the new country. The opposite also tends to be true. If one has been forced to come because of war, famine, persecutions and so on, there may be more resistance to the new culture. In some cases, however, this is offset by a determination to survive and the reality of never being able to return to one's homeland.

Intent to stay in the United States. Naturally if a newcomer does not intend to stay in the U.S. permanently, there is a lower level of motivation to make adjustments in behavior to approximate the U.S. culture.

Ha was influenced to some extent by each of these factors. The adaptation of his objective culture, however, is not the same as his becoming "American." It takes more than outward similarities to have another culture. It is easy to confuse this visible change with actually changing one's culture.

Understanding that objective culture can change without any change in subjective culture is an important concept to remember when building relationships across cultures.

Third Culture
A growing body of research is being done on what is being called "third culture."[6] A third culture develops when children grow up in a family of one culture, but in a larger society of a different culture. Second generation, American-born, 1.5 generation[7] all refer to the third culture phenomenon.

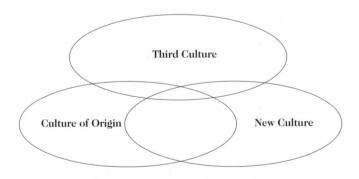

Figure 1.2. Development of third culture

As figure 1.2 indicates, the second generation immigrant forms a unique, third culture by combining the parents' culture with the new culture. The result is a culture that reflects a mixture of values and beliefs that reflect only a portion of their two, strong, primary cultural influences. The combination will reflect aspects of each primary culture as well as the individual's own special blending of those cultural patterns. By analyzing a person's cultural beliefs and behaviors, one can identify aspects of the person's culture of origin, the new culture and those that seem to be unique to a third culture person.

Second generation Americans may share common experiences that more closely link them to each other than to a first generation person of their same cultural heritage. For example, if the children learn English faster than the parents, they may take on responsibilities in the family that are beyond their age, contributing to feelings of isolation and loss of childhood. Common experiences such as these provide strong bonds and similar values that serve as a common third culture affinity.

Recognizing the uniqueness of a third culture helps in understanding and forming meaningful relationships.

Cultural Assimilation

For many in the United States, the talk of assimilation (the process of cultural values and behaviors becoming like that of another culture's) is anathema. For others, generally from the dominant culture, to resist assimilation seems ludicrous. They ask, "Why would someone come to the United States if they did not want to fit in?"

From a cultural perspective assimilation represents the death of one's heritage and identity. No matter where people live, they are generally proud of their heritage and cultural background. Most of us tend to live and associate with persons of similar heritage, reinforcing from generation to generation our values and traditions. Our culture may change, as in fact all cultures do at differing rates of speed; but to have our culture assimilated into another would be a catastrophic loss of heritage and identity.

In simple terms, cultural change is influenced by historical events, the arts, the economy, science and technology. Think about the cultural changes in the United States over the last twenty years. Values and beliefs have shifted. Though all cultures change, some cultures, such as that of the United States, change quickly. Other cultures, for example that of Thailand, change more slowly.

Assimilation, on the other hand, refers to something other than a natural evolution of cultural change. The process of assimilation deals with persons of one culture taking on the cultural characteristics of another culture. While this can happen over time and throughout generations, it can also be something that is forced on one group by another. The assimilation process for many Native Americans has caused them to lose their language and traditions. Forced assimilation can have devastating consequences and history shows it has led to violence.

True assimilation may take many generations and is not desired by everyone who lives in the United States.

Some in the field of crosscultural studies believe that it takes at least four generations to completely assimilate. The variables in this process are similar to those factors influencing the adaptation of objective culture. Some reasons families assimilate may be obvious, such as intercultural marriages, economic incentives, commu-

GENERATIONS

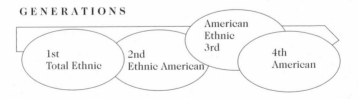

Figure 1.3. Process of assimilation. Oscar Romo, presentation to Language Missions Leadership Conference, Los Angeles, February 23-26, 1990.

nity pressure or isolation from others of their culture. The reasons others maintain strong cultural ties may also seem apparent: close-knit families, self-sustaining economic structures, strong ties to their country of origin and so on.

Stereotypes and Archetypes

Once contacts are made crossculturally, usually one of two paths is taken. We either begin to form or confirm stereotypes, or we begin to construct archetypal frameworks. It is important to know and understand the differences between these two approaches to categorizing cultural information. Notice what happens with Mary Beth.

Mary Beth works as a salesperson in a local department store that recently hired several Koreans. Mary Beth observes that these Koreans speak only to each other unless they are with a customer, and then only to answer the customer's specific question. After a few days Mary Beth comments to her family, "Koreans are cliquish and must not like Americans."

Mary Beth is beginning to develop a stereotype of Koreans. With her limited exposure to Koreans, she forms an opinion about all Koreans. The more obvious the differences between people, the quicker the tendency to form stereotypes.

Stereotypes have three characteristics. They are
☐ from an outsider's perspective, that is, someone not from that culture
☐ restrictive or limiting
☐ accusative[8]
Stereotypes originate with someone making an observation about members of another group. Often the observation is true of the few people observed and may even point out a positive quality, but to generalize that quality to all the members of the group creates a box, which limits the way in which others of that group will be seen. It allows people outside the group to decide who the others are without having to consider who that individual person is. Ethnic jokes and nicknames develop from these stereotypes. These

comments are never appropriate. Many times people believe that ethnic jokes are OK as long as they heard them from someone from that ethnic group. This, however, is not true. Ethnic jokes, derogatory comments and idioms that are based on a stereotype create barriers to real relationships.

Mary Beth can respond differently. She can begin to learn about Korean culture from someone within the Korean culture and so develop a general idea of Korean values and beliefs. With this archetypal approach she would learn that Koreans who are not very comfortable speaking English will not want to "lose face" by making mistakes. (The concept of losing face will be discussed in more detail later, but simply stated it refers to a sense of shame that one has not lived up to an expectation.) She would therefore have information about an important part of Korean culture (losing face) and gain a better understanding of her coworkers. She could then interpret the behavior she sees in light of her new knowledge of Korean culture.

Archetypes allow a person to have a general idea of cultural norms, customs and values without limiting anyone to be the archetype. An archetype is developed by an insider and is non-accusative and non-restrictive.[9]

Speaking about my own culture, I could say that U.S. Americans are generally individualistic. I know that may not accurately describe all persons of the dominant U.S. culture, but it is my perception, and if corroborated by a majority of U.S. Americans, would be considered part of our archetype.

While I may know many Koreans and may feel I know a great deal about Korean culture, I will never be Korean. My observations about Koreans should be exactly that—observations about the Koreans I know. To move beyond that to believing that all Koreans act a certain way based on my outsider perspective, is to stereotype Koreans. No matter how many Koreans I know, my experience is significantly less than any Korean's would be. I am only able to view Korean culture through my own cultural lenses and limited experiences that may distort what I see. As we look later in detail at some other cultures, the statements made will be archetypes provided to help give a framework for understanding cultures.

Archetypal models will help you avoid stereotyping and make for better relationships in a multicultural world.

Misattribution

While the example of Mary Beth shows how stereotypes are formed, it also lays the groundwork for the biggest problem in multicultural relationships: "misattribution." By definition, misattribution is "attributing meaning or motive to someone's behavior based upon one's own culture or experience."[10] If you have had any contact at all with someone from another culture, one, if not both of you, has probably been guilty of misattribution. While misattribution is common to all cultures, it may happen more often and be less corrected in the dominant culture of an area because there is less incentive to try to discover other alternative explanations. Misattribution is often hard to recognize because of two factors. First, our cultural beliefs are so ingrained that they appear to be either common sense or universal. Secondly, misattributions often evoke an instant emotional response. Little thought is then given to the accuracy or origin of the belief that prompted the feelings. The following three examples illustrate how important it is to discover misattributions.

Example 1. Two women, representing committees of different cultures, met to discuss working together in the future. Jo is Native American and Sue is Anglo-American. When the conversation ended, they each interpreted the encounter to a person of their own cultural background. Jo said that Sue had presented some good ideas that she would like to consider implementing. She was not sure if she got all of the information needed because Sue spoke very fast and was eager for Jo to commit to the project. Jo reported that she was afraid that there were some drawbacks that only time would help them see. She advised being cautious as they moved ahead.

Sue related to her friends that she was quite frustrated with her encounter with Jo. She observed Jo sitting quietly with her arms crossed, obviously resistant to the new approach. No matter how hard she tried to encourage her to ask questions and express her concerns, Jo would only listen and give vague responses. Sue believes that there is no hope that Jo will agree to pursue the joint project.

Note how the behavior of each woman was interpreted through her own cultural lens. If each woman had understood more of the other's culture, the understanding of the conversation may have been quite different. Jo would understand that for some Anglo-Americans their rate of speech is most indicative of where they grew up and does not mean that they are trying to be unclear, pushy or domineering. In addition, knowing that Sue's culture is results oriented, Jo could have been prepared that Sue would expect some kind of commitment when the conversation ended. This small amount of information would have enabled Jo to avoid her misattributions.

Likewise, if Sue had understood Jo's culture, her conclusions would have been altered. In Jo's culture it is respectful to sit quietly while someone is speaking and it is considered wise not to make a commitment too hastily. Knowing this cultural information would have given her the ability to interpret the encounter with a totally different meaning.

Example 2. Two pastors met at a conference and introduced themselves. The first one said, "Hello, I am Ralph Jones, pastor of the Downtown Christian Church." His new acquaintance said, "It is nice to meet you. I am Pastor Jong Kim, the pastor of First Korean Church in Scottsdale." While having lunch together, they ran into a colleague of Reverend Jones.

Ralph introduced his new Korean friend, "Jong, I would like you to meet John, an old friend of mine from college."

Placing his hand on Jong's shoulder, he continued, "Jong is a fellow pastor whom I have just met." Although Pastor Kim said nothing, he felt disrespected. A misattribution led to this feeling.

In Reverend Kim's culture pastors are shown a great deal of respect and are always introduced and referred to by a title. This title could be doctor (if they have a degree), pastor or reverend. To be treated in a familiar way by a person he barely knew, as Pastor Jones was, communicated disrespect. He did not consider that in Ralph's culture familiarity may not indicate lack of respect. In fact, in Ralph's culture, his friendliness and warmth to Pastor Kim expressed his genuine desire to be friends.

Example 3. I walked into a seminar class as the teacher. I made my introductory remarks in a subdued tone, making eye contact with no one. I used no hand gestures, but rather held my hands straight to my side. After only a few minutes the class made some decisions, based on their culture, about me as a teacher.

Those participants from the U.S.-dominant culture would probably have concluded one or more of the following: I was boring, unprepared, nervous, shy or just an inadequate teacher. However, those who were Laotian would see my behavior differently, concluding that I was a respectful and admirable teacher. Both audiences would have interpreted my behavior through their own cultural lenses.

From the time we are born, we begin to develop a process for interpreting behavior—a cultural lens through which we understand our surroundings. It is taught to us by our parents and community and soon becomes intuitive and automatic. This shorthand is a great skill and enhances our ability to function in the world around us, unless that world is made up of more than one culture. In the latter case our shorthand actually handicaps us, because we misread others' behaviors and end up believing the wrong message.

If this book does nothing else but help you see the dangers of misattribution, it would have been worth reading, for I believe this may be one of the biggest sources for poor relationships across cultures.

There are several precautions and remedies for misattributions.

☐ Learn about your own culture's values and behaviors.

☐ Learn about the specific culture with which you are working.

☐ Learn to check things out by asking a "cultural coach," that is, someone from the culture you are working with who will help you understand the culture and give you guidance on specific issues.

☐ Learn ways to talk about culture and its impact on your relationships with your friends from other cultures.

☐ Learn to ask yourself, "On what am I basing my feelings and thoughts about this relationship?" Make sure you are not basing them on a misattribution.

Misattributions are easy to make and can be a factor in relationships even when we are not aware of them.

Connecting

To become connected to your community, try one or more of the following projects.

1. Take out your local telephone book. Pick some common ethnic names and see how many are listed. Look up physicians. How many have names that appear to be of an ethnic origin other than your own? Try looking at restaurants, other than ethnic chains. How many and what kind do you see? Are there import/export stores? What signs of other cultures in your community can you find, for example, mosques, temples, non-English newspapers, radio and television programs and so on?

2. Rather than absent-mindedly driving familiar paths through your city, pretend everything is new to you. What do you see? What are some of the stores you see? Who helps you at restaurants, hospitals, convenience shops, computer stores and parking lots?

3. Go to the library and read several different newspapers from the same day. What do they tell you about the world around you? What are the cultural issues facing our world, our nation, your state and your city? While you are there, check out some books on culture. You will find a list in the suggested readings at the end of this book.

4. Check your telephone directory to see if there are any refugee resettlement offices in your community. If there are, give them a call and find out the countries of origin for the refugees being settled in your community.

5. Read your local newspaper or listen to a news broadcast. Find a story describing a conflict between two or more culture groups. Are there any misattributions? What advice would you give the parties in the conflict?

6. Think about a culture group with which you have had an experience. What do you believe about that group? Are these beliefs stereotypes? Are these beliefs based on misattributions? Check with someone or a book on that culture to see what the archetype would be.

7. List the culture groups in your community. Do not forget the ones who may look just like you.

2.

Do You Understand
Your Own Culture?

*"The future of America 'In a globalized economy without a cold war will rest
with people who can think and act with informed grace across ethnic,
cultural, and linguistic lines. And the first step lies in acknowledging that we are
not one big world family, or ever likely to be…in the world that is coming,
if you can't navigate differences, you've had it.'"*
ROBERT HUGHES

To begin a journey across cultures it is first important to take a look at yourself. You have a culture, learned values and behaviors taught by your family and community, but how do you know what about yourself is influenced by culture? If you were born in the United States, your cultural values will be influenced by the dominant U.S. culture. The extent to which you adhere to those values will be determined primarily by which part of the United States you and your family were reared, and your religious, ethnic and racial background. For the purpose of cultural research, the U.S. dominant culture is based on the U.S.-born, Anglo-Saxon middle class. Even if you fit that description, you might find that you are culturally different from the dominant U.S. cultural archetype.

Each culture has its ideal behaviors, its accepted or actual behaviors, and its unaccepted behaviors. The closer the accepted behaviors are to the ideals of a culture, the more static the culture, and in reverse, the farther the accepted is from the ideal, the more dynamic is the culture. In other words, static cultures are more uniform and change slowly, and dynamic cultures have more variations, or more microcultures (often referred to as subcultures or co-cultures), and will change more rapidly. Cultural anthropologist Darrell Whiteman illustrates this concept in figure 2.1.[1]

Figure 2.1. The correlation between ideal cultural behavior and cultural change

My neighbor, who was born in the United States, as I was, has physical characteristics and a language like mine, yet we do not have the same culture. Our cultural distinctiveness is not immediately visible, but it is profound. Neither of our cultures has an official name, but we acknowledge that we have different values, beliefs, and even to some extent, a different worldview. In general terms we are both part of the dominant U.S. culture, but in reality we belong to different subcultures within the larger U.S. culture. These more subtle subcultures or microcultures exist to some degree in almost all cultures, but cultures that have a steady flow of immigrants or large geographic areas are more apt to have greater cultural variation.

Our differences and stereotypes came to light when my neighbor and I began our first conversation. Our differences were noticeable from the moment we opened our mouths to greet each other. The way we sounded to each other shaped the way we received what the other was saying. My Texas speech pattern immediately indicated to my neighbor that I probably was not very bright and rather backward in my thinking. Her New York speech pattern told me that she was cold and aloof. We were both using stereotypes to make misattributions.

As people, we share a common human nature. Beyond that, our unique genetic makeup determines much of who we are. That is the "nature" part of us, or our birth characteristics. Our life experience, the "nurture" part, is just as complex as our genetic code. It involves our culture, gender, spiritual development, socioeconomic status, personal history, generational concerns, geography, phase of life, personality type and many other factors.

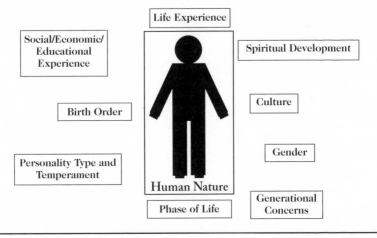

Figure 2.2. Culture box: Human nature and life experience

To understand ourselves, and ultimately our fellow humans, we must understand the influence of our culture on every aspect of who we are, how we think, how we interpret our experiences and what we value. It is as if you placed the culture box (see figure 2.2) and overlaid it on everything else in your life. Cultures have preferred personality types. The Myers-Briggs Personality Inventory is a self-testing instrument designed to reveal one's personality type in four categories: introvert-extrovert, intuitive-sensing, feeling-thinking, judging-perceiving. Studies done with this instrument indicate that cultural influences can be so strong that the percentages of personality types within a culture will vary, due in part, to what the culture values.[2] For example, in Australia the type ISTJ comprised 8.6 percent, while in Singapore it was 17 percent. In New Zealand the ESFJ type was 8.2 percent and in Pennsylvania, USA, the percentage was 13.97.[3]

Some cultures have preferred birth order and preferred genders. One's culture even shapes how we view our phase of life (single, married, married with children, empty nest, retired and so on).

Culture is not the only influence that shapes our behavior and values, but it is the lens through which all of life is seen and interpreted.

The following questions from Paul Pedersen and Allen Ivey's book *Culture Centered Counseling and Interviewing Skills*[4] will help you discover specific characteristics about your culture. Take time to answer each question by marking the number on the scale that most identifies your position between the two answers. Remember there are no right or wrong answers.

1. A person's identity lies within
the individual   1   2   3   4   5   6   7   the family
2. A person should place reliance on
others   1   2   3   4   5   6   7   self
3. A person learns from
personal experience   1   2   3   4   5   6   7   the wisdom of others
4. I am motivated by the need to
improve myself   1   2   3   4   5   6   7   be liked
5. I view other people's motives as
suspicious   1   2   3   4   5   6   7   basically trustful
6. I define friendship as including
many people   1   2   3   4   5   6   7   few people
7. In a social situation I feel that friendly aggression (teasing, one-upmanship and so on)
is acceptable and fun   1   2   3   4   5   6   7   embarrassing
8. I deal with conflict
directly   1   2   3   4   5   6   7   indirectly through others
9. I approach activity with a concern for
doing things together   1   2   3   4   5   6   7   being together

10. My usual pace of life is
fast, busy 1   2   3   4   5   6   7   slow, relaxed

11. I solve problems by
goal-based analysis 1   2   3   4   5   6   7   past knowledge or experience

12. I define time in terms of the
future 1   2   3   4   5   6   7   past

13. Nature is
mystical and fateful 1   2   3   4   5   6   7   physical and knowledgeable

14. I feel ultimately that what is desired can be achieved
if one works hard 1   2   3   4   5   6   7   in very limited measure

15. Youth should
show deference to wiser elders 1   2   3   4   5   6   7   lead progress

16. Feelings should be
suppressed 1   2   3   4   5   6   7   freely expressed

17. Personal beliefs should
conform 1   2   3   4   5   6   7   be asserted

18. In your life direction you should
follow a self-determined course 1   2   3   4   5   6   7   do what is needed of you

19. Problem solving should be
deliberate and logical 1   2   3   4   5   6   7   instinctive and impulsive

20. Manual labor is good for
the lower classes 1   2   3   4   5   6   7   anyone

21. With regard to the family
other relationships can 1   2   3   4   5   6   7   there is a strong
be just as important   loyalty and priority

22. Authority is
resented and rebelled against 1   2   3   4   5   6   7   respected and valued

23. The style of communication preferred is
tactful, indirect 1   2   3   4   5   6   7   open, direct

24. For the underdog, there is a feeling of
empathy 1   2   3   4   5   6   7   scorn

25. Elders receive
respect 1   2   3   4   5   6   7   disregard

❖   ❖   ❖

We will come back to these questions later in the book, but for now it will serve as a starting point to know yourself better and to begin to determine the influence of culture on your beliefs and behavior.

It is easy to believe that one's own culture is the best—because it works so well for you it seems impossible to think that it would not be best for everyone. The truth is that all cultures are equal in their ability to work for the people *of that culture*. Problems arise, however, when people from different cultures enter into relationships with each other and the beliefs long taken for granted are no longer shared.

Recently I taught at a conference titled When the World Lives Together. As part of our discussion I asked the class to identify what questions made them feel uncomfortable. I explained that in some cultures it was not uncommon, nor considered impolite, to ask someone how much they paid for an item.

Immediately one woman blurted out, "My mother taught me it was always rude to ask such a question." And her mother was right, for her culture. But the reality and challenge of a multicultural world are that we do not all have the same mothers.

Typically when faced with another culture, people will respond in one of the six ways described below. We must examine how we respond and discover how God would have us respond in our unique situations. It is also interesting to see if you respond one way to one culture and another way to a different culture.

Xenophobia

This refers to the fear of another culture. Such fear could be rooted in a number of causes, and may eventually evidence itself in racism, hate groups and crimes.

Roger lived in a small coastal town where the predominant occupations were related to the fishing industry. One day some newcomers arrived. They began purchasing boats and fishing in the same waters that Roger and his friends were fishing in. The competition became fierce because the market for fish was not enough to adequately support both groups of fishermen.

Because the newcomers were Vietnamese, the hostility became focused on their ethnicity and culture. Any misfortune that occurred in the town was blamed on the Vietnamese. Their traditions, values and ways of life were ridiculed. They were harassed when they shopped in the town. Violence even broke out on the docks. Both cultures began to fear each other and their fear was manifested as hate.

Ethnocentrism

This is the belief that one's own culture, race or ethnicity is the best. This is not the same as self-esteem or feeling good about who you are, but rather a belief in one's superiority to others. Ethnocentrism may display itself in patronizing or stereotyping other cultures and in seeing others as "tokens." As tokens, people are invited to be a part of the dominant culture, but not in a meaningful way. The most damaging reflection of ethnocentrism is bigotry and intolerance toward those who are different.

We have many examples of this attitude in Scripture, but let's look at Acts 10 for an example. In this passage Peter sees a vision of unclean foods and is told he should "kill and eat." This happens three times. While Peter is thinking about what this means, three men come to the house looking for him and asking if he would come with them to visit Cornelius, a God-fearing Gentile. This helped Peter understand the meaning of the vision and he knew that God would have him go with the men.

Why was this vision necessary? Didn't Peter want to share the good news with everyone? Actually, no. His Jewish culture gave him a limited perspective of cultures other than his own. God knew that it would take a dramatic event in Peter's life in order for him to see beyond his ethnocentrism.

We are not so different from Peter. Like him, we many times believe that our culture is better than any other culture or race. It is good for us to be reminded of verses 34-35 of this passage: "I truly understand that God shows no partiality, but in every nation anyone who fears him and does what is right is acceptable to him" (NRSV).

A church decided that they should elect a council member to represent the growing number of Hispanics joining the church. As the discussions on the topic grew, it became clear that the motivation was not to have genuine inclusion and representation but to give the illusion that there was representation. The Anglo church members wanted a token Hispanic to sit on the board. They particularly wanted someone who showed deference and loyalty to the church leadership, someone who would not expect changes. They felt justified in this position because they believed their church was great the way it was. Therefore to make any changes for Hispanic members would be weakening a strong church program. Proof of this belief was the fact that the Hispanic members had joined the church the way it was. The leaders felt justified in their approach. There was no animosity at all toward Hispanics or Hispanic culture, only the firm belief that the Anglo leadership knew what was best.

Forced Assimilation
Forced assimilation is a step away from ethnocentrism but still closely related to it, because at its root is the belief that one's culture is the best, therefore everyone should be "like me." However, with this position the person welcomes the other culture as long as the others will assimilate. In other words, "They can be on my team if they play just like I do."

At times this approach can seem quite friendly and may be motivated by a desire to be helpful. Many of the early advocates of integration held strongly to this belief, sincerely believing that it was best for all people and the country. "English only" laws reflect this same perspective.

Again if we look to Scripture, we see the same attitude expressed in the Judaizers—who were willing to accept Gentile converts as long as they would become Jews (see Acts 15). How often do we express that same mentality on issues without really being aware of what we are doing?

Martha volunteered at her church as a teacher of English as a Second Language (ESL). She enjoyed her relationships with her students and took a great deal of personal interest in them and their families. She involved the internationals in shopping trips, museum visits and church functions. She was always thinking of ways to include her students in her daily life. Her goal was to have them, at their own initiative, join in the functions she found so rewarding and fulfilling. She did not dislike their cultures but rather ignored them altogether. She did not patronize or believe she was better than her new friends, but believed it was in their best interests to abandon their cultures as quickly as possible and become "like an American." Everyone at the church admired her commitment and sacrifice for her new friends. In fact, she was often praised and cited as an example of what the church would like to see from all the volunteers.

Martha was doing many things well in her relationships with her international friends; however, her friendships centered on the Americanization of her students. Rather than building relationships based on mutual learning and shared experiences, Martha was expending her energy on teaching her friends her own culture, values and language. She was confident that she was doing what was best for her friends by helping them to become "American" as fast as possible. *After all,* she thought, *they are living in the United States now.* She truly wanted them to fit into the community.

Martha was not wrong in being a cultural guide for these newcomers, exposing them to the lifestyles and values of their new environment. Because Martha was proud of her culture and wanted her friends to adapt quickly, she did not call attention to any negative aspects of U.S. culture. Even though she truly cared for her friends, it was a care based to some degree upon her ability to help them become more like her. Martha believed that she was helping her friends in exactly the way they wished. Martha confused the international students' desire for a relationship with their desire to change their culture. By making such strong efforts to change her friends, there was a subtle message of "Your culture is not okay."

To put this in another perspective, let's assume that Martha is Anglo and that she is working with an African American woman on a team at work. How would her subtle messages of needing to be more like the dominant culture be perceived? In Martha's mind she is trying to be helpful, maybe even a mentor. But how would the other woman feel? What would she understand the message to be?

Segregation

Segregationists believe that different races and culture groups should remain separate from each other. This was a popular view prior to the civil rights movement when the premise of "separate but equal" was revealed to be separate but not equal. Currently some ethnic and racial leaders, such as Louis Farrakhan, are reviving this belief. They believe that only leaders of one's particular culture can give appropriate guidance to a group and therefore must be allowed to do so in separate venues. Evidence of this is the increased demand for "African American only" schools.[5]

Acceptance

Others are willing to show acceptance of other cultures. They are willing to coexist, accommodate and build relationships with those of other cultures. There is a recognition that all cultures are equal and should be respected. This is a worthy goal. Many diversity training programs in the business world advocate acceptance and tolerance within their multicultural teams. Acceptance is good but God calls us to do more.

Celebration

Celebration is characterized by valuing other cultures because God created us as cultural beings and values diversity in all of creation. This attitude appreciates mutuality in relationships and the desire for multicultural experiences and relationships. Celebration extends beyond accepting and tolerating to embracing and valuing.

A local church began to recognize that its area was changing demographically, and it wanted to respond to the challenge of being a church that would truly be inclusive of the entire community. As new families came into the church great effort was made at matching their talents and gifts with places of service. In so doing the church found leaders from several cultures. Now the task became incorporating different styles of worship, each with meaningful function and tradition, in order to reflect honest, indigenous worship and to celebrate the glory of God's redemption for all humankind. The church members faced many struggles as they intentionally kept focused on becoming the church that God wanted them to be in their community. Their strength came from their dependence on God and their recognition that no one culture has the corner on truth. Together they could be stronger than any one of them would be alone.

Culture and the Church
As you read these definitions did you see yourself? Are you responding to persons of other cultures as you want to be? As you study the New Testament, what response do you see from Jesus? How do you think he would want you to respond?

The U.S. Christian community has not taken the lead to endorse the acceptance and celebration of other cultures. Churches, rather than being outspoken on issues of racial justice and equality, have typically been silent or even worse, supportive of segregation. This has not improved as immigrants to the United States have become more noticeable. Why would this be so, when Christians have led the way in humanitarian efforts around the world? Have we been blinded by our culture to the challenge set before us as followers of Christ and celebrators of his creation?

When our way of life or our standard of living feels threatened, in general, Christians respond like the rest of their society. Our desire to protect those priorities supersedes the knowledge that we have of Christ's teaching related to how we should value and treat our neighbors. In fact we are so much a part of our U.S. cultural values that we seldom see the contradictions between the standards we profess and the values we protect.

In the days following the September 11, 2001, terrorist attacks on the World Trade Center, a church that was sharing its building with a Middle Eastern congregation decided to remove the sign that indicated that the Middle Eastern church met on their property. The Anglo church's perspective was that having this visible sign on their property might make them targets for graffiti, vandalism or even a more serious hate crime. They reacted to the unfolding news of terrorists attacking the United States as the general public did. Their fear of being retaliated against for allowing this church to meet in their building led them to make a decision based out of their culture rather than their faith. The strong cultural values of materialism (wanting to protect their physical property and their financial well-being), individualism (responsible to take care of one's own first) and even privacy (it is no one's business who we have meeting here) motivated their decision.

It was only after seeing their action through the perspective of the Middle Eastern congregation that some realized which values they had given priority. For the Middle Eastern church, the Anglo church's decision was one of denying them as their brothers and sisters in Christ. Both churches believed they were one body in Christ, yet removing the sign in a time of crisis reflected the Anglo church's decision to go with their culture rather than their theology.

The Middle Eastern congregation, which faces the potential for retaliation and harm each day it publicly proclaims Jesus as Lord and Savior, was surprised that their sisters and brothers in Christ would so quickly hide their relationship. Both congregations learned a valuable lesson on the blind spots culture can create and how we need others' eyes to point these out as we journey together in Christ.

For example, when African Americans moved into predominantly Anglo neighborhoods, most churches resisted along with the rest of the Anglo community. Their justification was the same as that of the non-Christians, and even worse, they tried to use the Bible to support their fear of living in close proximity to a culture different from their own. Even today it is often observed that the most segregated hour of the week is 11 a.m. on Sunday.

Knowing how you would like to respond to other cultures will help guide you as you learn how to engage a multicultural world.

Connecting

1. Go back and look at the inventory you took. How would you see Jesus responding to each question? On what are you basing your answers?

2. Our cultural values can be seen in our idioms or common expressions. Write down five idioms from your culture and what value each teaches.

For example:

☐ "He pulled himself up by his own bootstraps," shows a value of independence and self-reliance.

☐ "It takes two to tango," shows a value of taking responsibility.

You may also want to ask others of your culture to give you five idioms and determine the value taught in each. (This is also a good conversational tool in a crosscultural conversation.)

3. Many cultures have similar values and words of wisdom. See if you can match these U.S. idioms to their Chinese counterparts.

1. Biting off more than you can chew.	A. To blow on the hair and search for tiny sores.
2. The truth will win out.	B. The horse that leads the herd astray.
3. A drop in the bucket	C. If one plants melons, one gets melons.
4. Picky, picky, picky.	D. Like ants on the top of a hot cooking pot.
5. As you sow, so shall you reap.	E. Riding a tiger and finding it hard to get off.

6. The bad apple that spoils the barrel.

F. One hair from nine oxen.

7. On pins and needles.

G. Paper cannot wrap up fire.

4. Think about your everyday world. What culture groups do you have contact with and how would you categorize your response to them? Review the six responses listed (pp. 37-42). Do you respond differently to different cultures? Why? What response would God have you to make?

5. Think about the influences on who you are. In figure 2.3, fill in each box for yourself to form your visual autobiography.

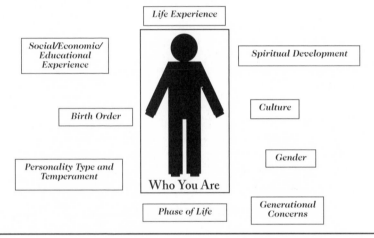

Figure 2.3. Visual autobiography

6. As you think about the box in figure 2.3 that is labeled culture, list the influences on your culture. This includes historical information about your country of origin or the persons in your family who have influenced your values and likewise the cultural influences on them. (For example, my mother grew up in the northeastern United States, and many of her values are consistent with the culture of that region. Although I grew up in the South, my mother's values are part of my unique cultural heritage.)

7. Respond to the following statements by determining whether they are universal truths (true for everyone regardless of culture) or whether they are molded by culture.

Table 2.1. Universal truths or culturally determined truths

Statement	Universal Truth	Culturally Conditioned
1. People should always strive to arrive at the appointed time.		
2. It is best to tell a person if they have offended you.		
3. Women should not wear makeup.		
4. It is rude to accept an offer if only asked once.		
5. It is better to be rich than to be poor.		
6. One should choose one's own spouse.		
7. Polite men will allow women to walk through doorways first.		
8. Being a good citizen means agreeing with your country's leaders.		
9. Individuals have the right to make decisions about their future, regardless of what their family wants.		
10. Good children will agree with their parents.		

8. Discuss your responses with people of different generations and different cultures. Write down your reactions to your discussion.

Answers to question three:

1. E	3. F	5. C	7. D
2. G	4. A	6. B	

Answers to question seven:

All of these are culturally based.

3

Where Are We?
The Importance of Context

"It's true that moral guidance and counsel need to be given,
but the way you say it and to whom you say it are as important as what you say."
1 TIMOTHY 1:8 THE MESSAGE

To begin crossing cultures, we need to examine the "lenses" of culture. Each culture has a unique way of seeing life and relationships. When we understand our own cultural lenses and the lenses of others, we are more likely to make friends with persons of other cultures. These lenses will provide a framework through which we can understand and build healthy crosscultural relationships.

There are six dimensions of culture that provide cultural lenses necessary for understanding the specific aspects of any culture. Learning these aspects of culture and understanding how they apply to your relationships is the major focus of the next six chapters. Through this process you can begin to develop meaningful and enriching crosscultural relationships.

Before we begin, let's review how culture is defined: "a system of meanings and values that shape one's behavior." Even those who have a great deal of experience working with other cultures may find it difficult to distinguish between culturally-based and personality-based behaviors. Ideally one should have a cultural coach who can answer specific questions and help you know which of these you may be dealing with. If no coach is available, the following are some good general questions to ask yourself.

1. Are your observations common to other persons of that same culture?

2. Do you find that same behavior (in similar circumstances) in persons who are not from that culture?

3. What is the response/reaction of others from the same culture to the behavior?

4. Is there any aspect of culture (which you will learn about in this and following chapters) that would support your belief that this behavior is cultural?

5. Is this behavior consistent and does the person appear to treat it as normal, natural behavior in the given circumstance?

Crossing cultures is easier when one understands which differences are culturally based and which are not.

Cultural differences are real and significantly influence our crosscultural relationships.

Context
The first lens to enhance cultural understanding is context, comprising of high context and low context. Edward T. Hall in *Beyond Culture* identifies context as an important aspect of cultural understanding because different cultures relate to the context of life in a variety of ways.[1] Low context cultures place a small amount of importance on the context while high context cultures place a large degree of meaning on the context.[2] Context includes

☐ environment (setting, location, decorations and so on)

☐ process (*how* the meeting is conducted, *how* participants were invited and so on)

☐ body language, facial expression and tone of voice (body language is not a universal language, for example, a gesture in one cul-

ture can mean something very different in another culture)
☐ appearance (clothes, jewelry and so on)

High Context Cultures
High context cultures operate on the following assumptions:
☐ The context of an event is as important as the event itself.
☐ "The listener is responsible for understanding communication."
☐ There is "no distinction between the idea and the person."
☐ Experience is equal in value to fact.
☐ Life is viewed holistically.[3]

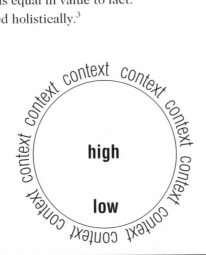

Figure 3.1. The context lens comprises high and low context

The context of an event is as important as the event itself.
Where and how something is done determines to a large degree
what is truly communicated. The context—environment or setting—has great value and meaning to these cultures; they have a
high regard for context. This is not unlike reading someone's body
language to either validate or invalidate what the person is saying.
For example, if I say, "This really tastes good," but at the same time
my facial expressions indicate I am having a hard time swallowing
it, you would probably believe what my facial expressions communicate rather than my words.

It works the same way for high context cultures. They look at the context of an interaction to see if what is being said is true. The assumption is that it is always possible that there is another message "between the lines" of communication. When a high context person is working with a low context person, the cues being read may be totally misleading. Rather than gaining a more accurate interpretation of the event, a less accurate one is being received.

Reverend Takarada, a local Japanese pastor, has been chosen as the recipient of the New Church Award. The presentation ceremony is scheduled for the last meeting of the year. Reverend Takarada has been notified well in advance that he will receive this award and will be asked to make a brief acceptance speech. This Japanese pastor prepares several hours for his speech, and on the day of the event, brings his wife and children to the ceremony.

The chair of the awards ceremony has prepared as usual for the event. The meeting is in the fellowship hall of one of the larger churches in the area. There are no decorations on the table and lunch is self-service. Reverend Takarada is the only one in a suit. No seating arrangements have been made for him or for his family. The format is casual and includes a great deal of humor. Reverend Takarada accepts his award and makes his speech, but is uncomfortable that most are still eating and not paying attention. He leaves the meeting very quietly and does not return to the pastors' conference meetings for many months. No one understands why he seemed so offended at receiving an award.

The answer lies in understanding the importance of context in Japanese culture. While Reverend Takarada was grateful to receive the award, he was confused when the award ceremony was handled in such a seemingly informal way. If the ceremony planners had known the importance of context to Reverend Takarada, they could have made a few adjustments in the program that would have demonstrated their respect to the honoree.

The International Friendship program at Central Church was preparing a special celebration for the graduates of the English as a

Second Language course. The women graduating had worked hard and represented five different Asian countries, including Japan and Korea. As the teachers were making preparations, they learned that the fellowship hall was already booked on graduation night. Because they did not want to change the night of the celebration, they decided to use a large classroom area that was available. The teachers making the arrangements were excited to have the celebration and wanted everything to be very comfortable for the women who were graduating. They decided to have a casual atmosphere so that the women and their families would enjoy being in church and might feel more inclined to return.

Many Asian cultures, including Japan and Korea, are high context cultures. With what you just read about high context cultures, can you guess the feelings of the guests that night? Remember that for high context cultures the setting or context of an interaction will be as significant as the interaction itself. What did the church inadvertently communicate through the context of the event?

Unless the guests understood U.S. dominant culture well enough to know that a casual evening of refreshments without speakers, gifts or flowers was still a celebration, they might not have felt very honored. If the teachers had understood the importance of context, they could have planned a more formal evening with a special speaker, flowers on the tables, small gifts for the graduates and so on, in order to communicate clearly the admiration and love they really felt for the graduates.

Many times I am asked to visit congregations whose culture is very different than mine. Before I go, I need to know where the majority of the people, and specifically the pastor, are on the lens of context. This particular piece of information will help me know how to begin to process the event, starting with how to dress. When I attend an African American church, I will dress in a suit or nice dress and heels, because the context of worship in this community is high. For a postmodern congregation context is also important, but to fit in there, I need to dress casually.

High context will not always mean formal, but it will mean that one must pay attention to the context. This does not mean that if I came dressed differently to either of these services I would be rejected or criticized. However, it does mean that if I want to have one less barrier in building relationships, I need to understand the importance of context, and if context is important, to discover what is considered appropriate for the situation I will be in.

The second assumption of high context cultures is that the listener is responsible for the communication. In other words, if the listener misunderstands what is being said then it is the listener who has failed, not the speaker. The implications here are numerous. Think about your own conversations and presentations. Are you a person who asks, "Am I making sense?" or "Is everyone following me?" If you are from a high context culture, you probably do not do that. Your assumption is that it is the listeners' responsibility to understand. To ask if they understand would be embarrassing to them.

If, as a high context person you are learning English, you may wonder if you are pronouncing words correctly or using the right word in a particular sentence. If you question whether your listeners understand you, such questioning reflects your desire to know whether you are using the right word, rather than whether the listener understands.

Yi Ling had been in the United States for only three months when she enrolled at the university. Because she was not confident about her English skills, she asked to be assigned a tutor for her English class. The tutor was very impressed with Yi's comprehension and ability to follow instructions. However, when the grades on the first exam were posted, she was shocked and disappointed to learn that Yi had barely passed.

In their next session she questioned Yi about what had happened. Yi began to cry and left the session. Later Yi asked to be assigned a new tutor. Before making a new assignment, the faculty supervisor of the tutoring program asked Yi to come by for a visit.

In the interview the advisor asked many questions, especially about what her educational experiences had been like in China and how students and teachers interacted. After a long discussion it became clear that the problem had not been Yi's ability or the tutor's knowledge but rather their cultural differences.

When Yi was asked if she understood the lesson that the tutor had reviewed, she always replied "yes." She did not want to be disrespectful of the tutor nor did she want to admit her failure to understand. The tutor, unaware that this was a cultural behavior, took the responses literally. Yi expected her tutor to realize (as a tutor in her country would have) that she would need additional practice and review before truly grasping the concepts.

High context cultures assume that there is no distinction between the idea and the person. It is exactly this belief that often eludes international business people. Many times multinational business deals fall through because the corporate representative is believed to be untrustworthy, and not because the international partner does not want to participate.

One day a friend of mine from Pakistan came to my office experiencing deep depression and hopelessness. She had been quite ill. Her husband was experiencing difficulties at his work, as was she, and her children were leaving home to attend college. It seemed as if her life was totally out of control.

I recognized that I was not equipped to provide the kind of counseling that she would need, so we discussed her willingness to see a professional counselor. She was in agreement but did not know anyone from her culture in that field. I had several friends who were counselors, although I knew that none of them had very much experience with persons from other cultures. I decided to refer her to someone who did have experience with women about her age and with similar issues. The appointment was made, and I waited to hear her feedback on the session.

Within two weeks she returned to my office in tears after her first meeting with the counselor. The interaction she had with the counselor caused her to discount everything the counselor told her. Because she did not feel as if the counselor was kind or caring, she did not accept her suggestions nor did she want to return to see her. What the counselor had done was common practice and would have been seen as being professional by most U.S. Americans. But my Pakistani friend had made several misattributions that caused her to think that the counselor was unkind and uncaring. These misattributions were based on the context of the conversation and not the conversation itself.

Here is what happened. The receptionist, who did not engage in any small talk, required my friend to fill out many forms and detail much personal information before meeting the counselor. The professional, objective demeanor of the counselor was perceived as unfeeling. Her initial question, "How can I help you?" seemed rude and embarrassing. The counselor's office was decorated with modern art, which appeared cold and unfriendly to my friend.

When she was referred to another counselor, the results were totally different. This time there was no receptionist and no pre-visit paperwork. The office was homey in appearance, and to put my friend at ease, the counselor engaged in some personal conversation, such as talking about the origin of some of the knickknacks in her office. Although the two counselors made the same basic suggestions, my friend received the advice and felt helped by the second one. The context of the second counselor conveyed what the Pakistani client believed was consistent with a caring person whom she could trust.

In high context cultures, experience is equal to facts. Another way of saying this is that an experience, including one's interpretation of it, is a fact.

A nonprofit organization was doing work in many immigrant communities, one of which was the Korean community. After several years of this partnership, a large controversy arose concerning how the money allocated for Korean projects was being spent. While the administration of the organization produced records and audit reports, the Koreans were still not convinced that they had received their assigned portion. The problem stemmed from a distrust of one of the organization's representatives assigned to work with the Koreans. They perceived him to be untrustworthy and that *fact* was equal to the facts on the bank audit. In order to resolve the conflict, the organization had to address the Koreans' perception of the representative.

The fifth assumption of high context cultures is that life is holistic, seen as a whole. It is difficult for a high context person to view life in compartments. There is no work life, home life, social life or spiritual life, but rather life. The boundaries between these roles do not exist. This assumption underlies a great deal of what may seem baffling to low context persons.

Think about what is happening in this crosscultural work setting. A U.S.-born Anglo, Joe, supervises a Malaysian coworker, Peter. They have a good working relationship except when work needs revision. It is at this point that Joe feels trapped. He does not know how to tell Peter that changes need to be made to a project without having him overreact. Their dialogues go something like this.

Joe:	You did a great job on these plans. I really like them and I am sure the client will too. There is just one that I think you need to change. If you will [he describes the change], I think we can not only meet the requirements of the client but help out the budget as well.
Peter:	I see. I will do it right away. I am sorry I didn't do it as you wanted. I will do better next time.
Joe:	No, you did great. You always do good work and are very punctual in your projects. I will help you learn to adjust some of the estimates on the hardware so we can be competitive, that is where you are still weak. Make the changes I suggested, and we will submit the plans to the client.
Peter:	I will right away. Do you still want me on the project?[4]

Peter's holistic thinking led him to conclude that if he was unsatisfactory in one area he was unsatisfactory as an employee. He was not used to compartmentalizing his life and viewing his skills, behaviors and so on, as separate items. They were all him, so a deficit in one was a deficit in his whole being. This scenario plays itself out in many ways.

Think about the common U.S. Christian expression, "God loves the sinner but hates the sin." Do you think that this has much meaning to a high context thinker? Absolutely not. High context thinkers do not separate themselves into who-they-are and what-they-do categories. That type of analytical, compartmentalized thinking is low context thinking.

Low Context Cultures

Low context cultures have their own unique assumptions. As with high context cultures, these beliefs vary in degree and in application. Low context cultures believe:

☐ The content of the message is more important than the context.
☐ The speaker is responsible for the communication.
☐ They and others are defined by their recent achievements.
☐ Analytical thinking is preferred.[5]

The first belief is that the content of the message is more important than the context. Low context cultures do not use the setting or environment to filter or add as much meaning to interactions as high context cultures do. Low context cultures do not read subtleties well and do not necessarily look for them. This is in part why low context cultures value directness.

Both high and low context persons will seek a doctor who they believe is excellently qualified and personable. For a low context person, the doctor's credibility is based on credentials, good reputation and affiliation with a good hospital. Ultimately, of course, credibility is based on whether the doctor was actually of assistance.

If the patient is high context, many other factors will play a part in how the doctor is evaluated. Elements such as location of the office, attitude of the receptionist and nurse, and the doctor's style of communicating and demeanor will all be as important as the actual information received.

The context of an event can also refer to location. For example, where should business transactions take place? This answer is a function of one's cultural perspective of context. In the dominant U.S. culture (low context) very important agreements can be made on golf courses, in saunas or over lunch. In high context cultures, business in these settings would be considered inappropriate. Yet, in high context cultures, people use these social settings to get to know the persons with whom they are doing business—an important element of the transaction—so they can determine if the person is trustworthy. Thus, in high context cultures, socializing is the foundation for business, with formal transactions taking place in the appropriate business setting.

In low context cultures, the speaker is responsible for the communication. Now here are the same questions I asked before. Have you ever asked someone when speaking, "Am I making sense?" or, "Are you following me?" These are the questions of a low context person. If you are low context, you expect your listeners to feel free to tell you if they do not understand and you believe you have the responsibility to communicate in a way that others understand. As we have learned, this may not happen if your listeners are high context.

Neither of these approaches is inherently right or wrong. However, in order to communicate, it is vital to know that there can be a fundamental difference between high and low context cultures. If you are a high context person in conversation with a low context person, remember that you may be asked to clarify statements or concepts. This is not done to challenge your authority or knowledge, but rather to help you do what is thought to be your responsibility. If you are a low context person talking with a high context person, expect head nodding and statements of agreement, which may or may not indicate understanding. To check whether you are understood, ask for restatement or what the new information means to them.

Low context cultures define themselves and others by their recent achievements. This may be the most difficult difference to deal with in relationships because it is so subtle at times. Low context cultures appear to have short memories. They tend to be more fluid, accepting of and expecting constant change. Relationships are defined by "what you have done for me lately." High context cultures are much more likely to look at the whole history of the relationship rather than just the last few interactions.

Low context cultures prefer analytical thinking. In low context cultures life is looked at as many parts that make up a whole. A good example of this compartmental thinking was lived out on television. The media debated what action needed to be taken regarding President Clinton. Should he be punished in his political career for an act committed in his private life? The concept that there are private and public lives is a result of analytical thinking. It is interesting that even the proponents of impeachment did not deny the existence of Clinton's public/private life split. Rather, the argument centered on whether what he did in his private life should have consequences in his public life.

We saw the same compartmentalization of life in the previous illustration of Joe and Peter. It was Joe's ability to separate Peter's job performance into separate skills that enabled him to deal with Peter's work and not feel he was saying anything that was critical of him.

Understanding whether the person you are working with is a holistic or an analytical thinker will help you communicate in a meaningful way.

While the United States is a low context culture, there are situations in which context is extremely important. Consider the arena of religion. Here low context cultures do give meaning to context. The rituals, music and appearance are all part of the experience and add meaning to the experience. Funerals are another example where even low context cultures place meaning on the context. If you are low context and were bewildered by the reactions of the high context cultures in the previous illustrations, think how you would react if you were told that you should have your loved one's funeral in an amusement park!

One of the first things that should be done in building a crosscultural relationship is to discover whether the person's culture is high or low context. By missing this important aspect of culture the relationship can get off to a rocky start. For example, if you are a low context person (for example, from the dominant U.S. culture) and you are initiating a friendship with a person from a high context culture (for example, from Japan, some African American communities and so on), understanding the cultural context will be significant. Remember that for high context cultures the context is as important as the event itself. You, as the low context person, want to create ways to spend time together, maybe by shopping or running errands together. But if in doing so the other person feels lost in a shuffle of activity rather than the experience bonding the two of you, it will create a feeling of not being very important.

If you are a high context person trying to build a friendship with a low context person, you might err in creating too structured an environment for the person to feel relaxed and comfortable. Formal settings will communicate to a low context person that the relationship is based on roles or etiquette rather than a personal desire to be friends, and it will be harder for the person to be herself.

Knowing if a person is from a high or low context culture will assist you in preparing for multicultural events, meetings and communications.

Connecting

1. Would you classify your culture as high or low context? What examples can you think of that support your answer?

2. Refer to the questions in chapter two. Which ones reflect context?

3. Think of an experience you have had with a person from a culture different from your own. Was the person from a high or low context culture? Why do you think so? Would you be willing to talk to the person about the issues of context?

4. Make a chart that lists the attributes of high and low context cultures.

High Context	Low Context
1.	1.
2.	2.
3.	3.
4.	4.
5.	5.

5. If you were sharing your faith with a person from a high context culture, what would you do to accommodate what you have learned about high context culture? How would you accommodate a person from a low context culture?

4

What Drives Us?
The Value of Activity

*"When we are merely 'being ourselves,' acting according to our deepest instincts,
human beings reveal fundamental differences in what we all tend
to think of as normal behavior."*
CRAIG STORTI

In the previous chapter context was the lens we discussed. Now we will explore the *activity* lens.

The basic question of the activity dimension is: "How does the culture group define and perceive activity?"[1] Geert Hofstede's landmark study of cultural differences (1980) used the term *masculine* to describe the differences in the activity lens. Intercultural trainers Joanne Zitek and Cynthia Livingston, using Hofstede's cultural research, define Hofstede's two types as masculine cultures and feminine cultures.[2] In recent years it has seemed more meaningful to use *being* and *doing*, emphasizing the value rather than associating a cultural feature with a gender. Doing cultures value results and materialism. Being cultures value relationships and quality of life. For a ranking of countries on the doing/being scale, see figure 4.4 at the end of this chapter.

Figure 4.1. The activity lens

At first these two descriptions may appear to be a reflection of personality types rather than culture. In the Myers-Briggs Personality Inventory, part of the classification includes thinking versus feeling personality type. Both of these personality types reflect aspects of doing or being culture respectively, and can be found in almost all cultures.

However, our approach here is not to look at the variation of personality types within a culture, but rather the propensity for an entire culture to behave in ways that give more value to either being or doing. The U.S. culture, which is a doing culture, has persons who function within a large spectrum of behaviors, some appearing extremely doing-driven and others quite being-driven. When compared to a being culture, however, even someone who seems very being-driven will come across as a doing-driven person.

It is also possible for two people from the same culture to hold to the same value, but in a given situation express that value through different choices. The story of Mary and Martha in Luke 10:38-42 illustrates this point well. Mary seems to have been a being-driven person while Martha was a doing-driven person. However, remember that Mary and Martha had the same culture. What does their difference represent then? I believe that Martha was concerned with her tasks because she cared for her guest. To care for the relationship, she had to provide hospitality, which required her attention to household tasks. Mary too, wanted and valued relationships. She chose, however, to value the relationship with Jesus gained by listening to him over the relationship based on fulfilling a cultural role. Neither Mary nor Martha acted outside their cultural value of being, but Mary chose the way of relationship that had eternal value.

Figure 4.2 illustrates yet another confusing aspect of this lens. Notice that the United States's box is larger than the box representing Jordan. This reflects not population size but diversity within a culture. The United States has great diversity within the dominant culture, unlike Jordan, which historically has had a smaller number of immigrants and outside influences.

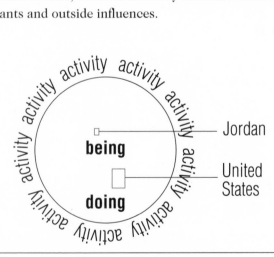

Figure 4.2. A comparison of being and doing cultures

The implications of doing and being cultures are significant. This cultural lens impacts how we value people, especially their activities and their gender roles. For doing cultures, activities that produce results are valued as are the people who are involved in those kinds of result-oriented activities. For being cultures, activi-

ties that enhance and build relationships are valued. A story of two
pastors may help demonstrate this principle.

Reverend Bill Williams serves as a mentor for new pastors. Because
of the large number of Arabic-speaking persons in their community,
Reverend Williams's church agreed to share its facilities with a new
Arab congregation. After only a few months, tension was evident in
their relationship. Each week when the two pastors met to share concerns and pray, the conversation would be something like this.

Reverend Williams:	How many did you have in worship on Sun-day?
Brother Ibrahim:	It was a great service. Praise God! God is really blessing us. Two new families came to our service.
Reverend Williams:	So how many were there in all?
Brother Ibrahim:	You must come and be with us sometime, pas-tor. Everyone is so excited. Our new music leader is doing a fantastic job with our wor-ship service. The people are praising God and I can tell that lives are really being changed.
Reverend Williams:	*(Frustrated, but trying one more time to get an answer to his question):* Did you notice how many people were there?
Brother Ibrahim:	Everyone stayed for our fellowship meal. We ate together and prayed for each other. Even our visitors had a wonderful experience.

On first reading this conversation, you might conclude that
Brother Ibrahim is resisting answering the question and that he is
avoiding it by talking about other things. Or you may think that
Reverend Williams is "hung up" on numbers and is not really listening to his fellow pastor tell him about the truly important aspects of
the church. Your culture largely influences how you view this conversation. The truth is that their doing and being cultures have col-

lided and neither one is acknowledging the other's values.

Brother Ibrahim's being culture has taught him to value relationships and the quality of life. When asked to give numbers, which are very important to doing cultures as a way of showing results, he does not have the numbers to give. Not only did he not count the people, he never *thought* to count the people. To him the numbers would not have meaning. What has meaning is what is actually happening with the people of his congregation.

Reverend Williams is frustrated in his relationship with his fellow pastor. He wants to be a good mentor to this young Arab pastor, but does not know what to do if Brother Ibrahim will not answer even a simple question. He cannot understand why it is so hard for him to provide a straight answer.

When Reverend Williams approached me about what he should do to make Brother Ibrahim respond to his question, I explained the cultural difference. As I was talking, the light seemed to come on for him.

Finally he said, "Oh, that must be why he always asks about my family and is so thoughtful of special occasions in the lives of our staff. We just thought he was trying to impress us." (Note the misattribution.) With this new cultural insight Reverend Williams has a choice to make. He can use this new information to try to motivate Pastor Ibrahim to report numbers by tying this to their relationship or he can change his approach to encourage him in the areas Brother Ibrahim does value.

I also spoke to Brother Ibrahim to see how he was feeling about the relationship. He, too, was frustrated but for an entirely different reason. He was concerned about Reverend Williams's spiritual condition. He wondered if the pastor was having some problems in his life that made him so worldly-minded. After he understood the cultural perspective of the pastor, he was able to change his misattribution to an accurate perception of what was actually happening. As the two came to a greater understanding of each other and each other's respective cultures, this potentially divisive difference did not destroy the relationship, but enhanced it. Both men were challenged to see the world through a broader lens.

Doing cultures do care about relationships and being cultures do care about results. It is the culture, however, that defines results and relationships. In being cultures results are seen from the perspective of relationship, and in doing cultures relationships are seen from the perspective of accomplishment.

In doing cultures, when the reason for the relationship changes it is acceptable for the relationship to change. No conflict need take place. For the most part relationships in doing cultures are seen as mutually beneficial and fluid.

What for many in a doing culture would seem codependent or unhealthy, in a being culture would be considered normal. In fact, interviews with foreign students indicate that one of their greatest sources of stress is the lack of relationships they find in the United States. In being cultures relationships are long-term and have a depth of commitment that is unusual for most people of the dominant U.S. culture. Many from being cultures experience coming to the United States like this international student who said, "It is like jumping into the cold water" to experience such a different sense of friendship.[3]

The U.S. culture is seen as friendly, but it is a shallow friendliness that can be very dependent on circumstances. In being cultures friendship is lifelong; it is not just the sharing of common activities but a commitment to be there for each other. As Robert Kohls, professor of cultural anthropology states, "The U.S. environment makes this kind of friendship extremely rare. . . . The mobility of people and the individualistic perspective not only make these relationships unusual, for many people they are not even desirable."[4]

If you work with people of other cultures in a business setting rather than a religious one, you may find the cultural differences between doing values and being values expressing themselves differently. Multicultural teams are common in many U.S. businesses today. While management may like the results these diverse teams can produce, the process of working together can be arduous. At times the conflict between doing and being priorities can create such tension as to make one wonder if the team approach is worth it.[5] In order to illustrate this let me take an example from a female work team.

The teaching staff of a public high school was asked by the administration office to form a team to make recommendations to the school board on disciplinary procedures for tardy students. Tardiness had become so prevalent that it was costing the school district thousands of dollars each year. They knew that the current policies were not effective and wanted the staff to have input into the solution.

The team was composed of tenured and nontenured faculty with teaching assignments in each field of study in the high school. Three of the women were U.S. born and the other two were born in Brazil and Vietnam respectively. From the very beginning there were obvious differences. The three U.S.-born women focused immediately on the fact that this problem was hurting their school's funding, resulting in their small salary increases the last few years. It was also causing disruptions in the classroom, impeding learning and lowering the test scores, again having a negative effect on them personally. They wanted to find a method of discipline that would have maximum effect as quickly as possible.

The teachers from Brazil and from Vietnam understood these ramifications, but wanted the team to understand what was causing the tardiness. They wanted to do something proactive to eliminate the cause of the problem. They were concerned about the quality of life for the students and felt a responsibility to the community as a whole to help fix the problem that was evidenced in the truancies. The U.S.-born teachers agreed in principle, but felt that it would take too long to see results from that approach. Moreover, it was not their assignment and they could not be responsible for fixing all the social problems affecting students.

The foreign-born teachers, both of whom came from being cultures, then faced a dilemma—whether to risk their relationships with their coworkers by pursuing their approach or risk letting their community down by not doing what they thought was best. The U.S.-born teachers also faced a decision—whether to compromise their efficiency and timely recommendation or risk alienating their counterparts. It was easy at this point for each group to feel it was right and criticize the other group for being shortsighted. However, the best solution was derived when these two aspects of culture were respected and valued. The team suggested to the administration that they report in phases: first, an immediate policy change with implementation, and then a study to determine the causes of the tardiness and possible systemic and proactive solutions.

Doing and being cultural differences affect our values and our priorities.

Connecting

1. Think about your culture in the area of doing and being. When you decide which one you think your culture is, decide where you are on the spectrum. For example, the United States is a doing culture, but within the U.S. culture would you be more doing or more being?

2. Think of how the activity dimension of culture influences you, your relationships, your priorities and your perspectives. Jesus lived here on earth as fully human and fully God. As fully human he was Jewish in his culture, yet his Jewish cultural values were challenged by what he knew to be the higher God-given standard. Many times we understand Jesus' behavior only after we understand the culture of his day, because he responded in accordance with those values. At other times it is clear that he is not responding out of his culture because instead of following the cultural norm he revealed a different way. Research the cultural beliefs at the time and then note which he was doing in the following passages:

☐ Jesus with the woman at the well, John 4:7-30.

☐ Jesus with the woman caught in adultery, John 8:1-11.

☐ Jesus and the Gadarene demoniac, Matthew 8:24-34

☐ Jesus and the Syrophoenician woman, Mark 7:24-30

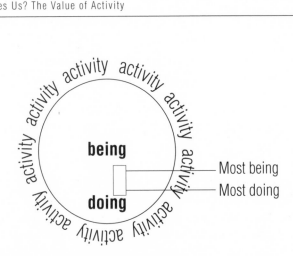

Figure 4.3. Rate yourself within your own culture

3. Think of situations where the two sets of values, doing and being, come into conflict. How would you try to resolve the conflict? Can you think of how working out the differences in perspective can actually bring about a better result than if you had started out with the same cultural value?

4. Read the following statements and decide whether you think the speaker was from a predominantly being or predominantly doing culture. Why do you think so?

    ☐ "While I was at the meeting, I made many new friends."

    ☐ "I don't think we got much done, but we all had a good time."

    ☐ "When she asked me to get involved, what choice did I have?"

    ☐ "I have lived here for thirteen years but I still don't have any friends."

    ☐ "I will need some help after my surgery so I will hire a nurse. I can't expect my friends to be able to come because they are all so busy."

Explanation

☐ "While I was at the meeting, I made many new friends." This statement is more likely to be made by a doing-culture person. It is the doing culture that calls relationships "friends" more casually and quickly.

☐ "I don't think we got much done, but we all had a good time." This statement is more likely made by a doing-culture person. You may have thought that it was a being culture, but most being-culture persons would not have even thought to say "we didn't get much done" especially if everyone had a good time. That would have been getting something done.

☐ "When she asked me to become involved, what choice did I have?" This statement is more likely made by a being-culture person. The commitment of friendship often means that an individual feels he/she does not have a choice of complying with a request—that is just part of the obligation of friendship.

☐ "I have lived here for thirteen years but I still don't have any friends." This statement is more likely to be made by a being-culture person. In being cultures, friendships take a long time to be seen as real friendships. After thirteen years in a place, most people from a doing culture would feel that they did have some friends. However, it is not uncommon for people from a being culture to feel friendless if they have been in a place with no other persons from their culture.

☐ "I will need some help after my surgery so I will hire a nurse. I can't expect my friends to come because they are all so busy." This statement is more likely to be made by a doing-culture person. While people from doing cultures acknowledge they have friends, they also recognize the boundaries of what one can expect of friends. Most being-culture persons would expect their friends to help them in this situation, believing that this is what friends do for each other.

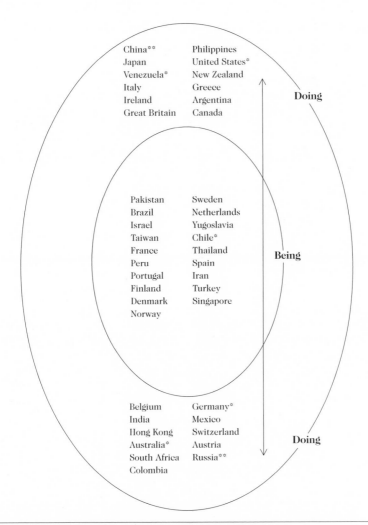

Figure 4.4. The doing/being lens. Geert Hofstede, *Culture's Consequences: International Differences in Work-Related Values* (Beverly Hills, Calif.: Sage, 1980), p. 315.

*These country categories changed during further research conducted by Denise Rotondo Fernandez, Dawn S. Carlson, Lee P. Stepina, and Joel D. Nicholson in "Hofstede's Country Classification 25 Years Later," *Journal of Social Psychology* 137, no. 1 (1997): 43.

**These countries were added in more recent research.

5 ◄ ....

Who's in Charge?
The Influence of Authority

"I was so surprised and confused when...the provost, in person,
held the door for me in order to let me pass before he would enter the door.
I was so confused that I could not find the words
to express my gratefulness, and I almost fell on my knees as I would certainly do
back home. A man who is by far my superior is holding the door for me,
a mere student and a nobody."
VISITOR FROM INDIA

T he authority lens addresses how a culture group defines and perceives authority. The two perspectives within this lens are egalitarian/informal and hierarchical/formal.[1]

Figure 5.1. The authority lens

Egalitarian Cultures

These cultures believe that all persons have equal value and equal rights. A culture may be egalitarian in its values and at the same time not treat each individual as equal. The United States is an egalitarian culture, with a constitution and Bill of Rights to confirm these values. And yet many in the United States are discriminated against and not given equal treatment. The fact that this unequal treatment is viewed by most U.S. Americans as wrong and shameful is actually a verification that the cultural value is that all people do have equal value and equal rights. Remember that the cultural ideal and actual behavior are not the same.

Hierarchical Cultures

In these cultures unequal treatment of persons is not only accepted but also expected and considered appropriate. Cultures with a high degree of hierarchy have rules for much of life and feel no cognitive dissonance with valuing persons differently according to gender, race, caste and so on. While every culture has its own protocol for certain occasions, hierarchical cultures rigidly adhere to their complex societal structures. For the individual member of a hierarchical society, failure to follow these cultural rules can bring severe consequences. These cultures tend to be high context cultures.

Of course, cultures vary in the degree to which they are either hierarchical or egalitarian. These differences can be visualized by placing them in between the center and the outer ring of the lens. In order to determine a person's degree of hierarchy, ask the question, "Who is able to be in leadership positions within your culture?" You might receive answers that vary from anyone with the skills (an egalitarian response) to only the men in a certain caste/family/tribe (a hierarchical response).

Another question to establish the degree of hierarchy would be, "Who is entitled to have authority over others?" If the person can easily rank people and the ranking has nothing to do with skills or training, the culture is hierarchical.

Members of the Community Christian Church were concerned about the large number of Asian Indians moving into the city. Their desire was to create an open atmosphere for relationships to begin and thrive. They sent out flyers, and in the stores frequented by Indians, they put up invitations announcing a fellowship for the entire community. They purchased a video in Hindi and tried to make the setting as attractive to their new neighbors as possible. Many Indians came but what the church members observed was surprising. All the Indians who attended spoke English very well and were able to speak with the church members in a sincere effort to make friends. However, they spoke very little among themselves, almost to the point of ignoring one another. The pastor asked me to help him understand why this had happened because it had not at all been what he expected.

My initial thought was that it had a great deal to do with hierarchy in the Indian culture. As we began to explore the demographic information of the Indians, we discovered that rather than this group being homogenous, they were in fact, extremely diverse and represented several castes, language groups and levels of education. While they were all comfortable visiting with the U.S. Americans, they did not have that same freedom among those from their own country. The hierarchy they had learned as children was very strong and still at work.

One day I received a very distressed call from the director of the international students at a nearby university. This was his first year in the position, but he had a real passion for internationals and had traveled extensively outside the United States. One of his first projects was to organize social events for all the international students. From the perspective of a doing culture (results-oriented), the events were very successful because the attendance was high. But this director wanted to look beyond the numbers to measure the success of the event. He was disturbed because the students, even those from the same countries, were not interacting with each other. From the perspective of a being culture (relational), the event was a failure, but the director did not know why.

We talked for a while and then I asked him, "What countries are the students from?" As he began to name them—India, Japan, Egypt, Peru, Venezuela, Germany, China, Brazil and so on—I recognized that most of these countries are strongly hierarchical. This information was critical in understanding why the students did not mingle. We decided that he should try to continue the events, but allow some time for each student to introduce himself/herself to the audience in a formal way. The students could then identify those with whom they would feel most comfortable. In addition, the formality and structure would allow them the opportunity to get to know about others whom they might not have ever have had the chance even to meet in their own countries.

Closely associated with the degree of cultural hierarchy is the extent of formality that the culture observes. There is a general correlation between high context cultures and hierarchical/formal cultures and low context and egalitarian/informal cultures. By informal, I mean that there is a casualness to society as a whole that is reflected in the acceptance of diverse ways of dressing, behaving, freedom to relate to others and to express oneself. The United States is becoming more and more an informal culture. Depending on your age, you may remember times when there were rules to govern what was appropriate and even who it was appropriate to associate with. The 1960s brought many changes, one of which was the relaxing of U.S. society's beliefs about uniformity and rules. "If it feels good do it" became the motto for many, a cultural belief which continues to grow stronger with each passing year. This approach to life makes it difficult for those of other more formal cultures to determine what is appropriate behavior, dress and so on. The informal nature of U.S. culture can also make it easy for one to be insensitive to the need others have for cultural uniformity and structure.

Egalitarian cultures are more informal and, as already stated, typically low context cultures. In the United States, an informal culture, one can go to a movie or a restaurant in a wide variety of attire and still be considered appropriately dressed. One can also be in a social setting with a wide spectrum of people and have no one think it strange. The beliefs of egalitarian and hierarchical cultures can be seen in many ways and can have many repercussions in our relationships.

Reverend Guiterrez has been asked to make a presentation to a group of new ministers about the Argentinean congregation that he pastors. While giving his address, Paul Smith thinks of a question that he believes would be of interest to the entire audience. He raises his hand almost as a wave and then begins to ask his question. While Reverend Guiterrez tries to answer the question, he is confused by his fellow pastor's rudeness. Pastor Smith feels sorry for the pastor because he assumes that Reverend Guiterrez is stumbling with his words because he does not know the answer.

What actually happened has a great deal to do with the assumptions and beliefs that have been described within the authority lens. Since he was invited weeks in advance to make a presentation, Reverend Guiterrez views the setting as formal. When he is asked a question during his presentation, he is confused. Why would Reverend Smith act so inappropriately? Why would he be so disrespectful? On the other hand, Paul Smith, who is from the dominant U.S. culture, sees the setting as informal—a group of pastors talking about their churches. He believes that his question will add to the presentation and be appreciated by the group because it gives Reverend Guiterrez an opportunity to expand some of his ideas.

What would have helped this situation? The person who arranged the program and invited Reverend Guiterrez could have done several things to avoid this situation. When she invited Reverend Guiterrez to speak, she could have explained that the audience would be very casual and that some might want to ask questions during his presentation. She could have further explained that a question and answer style of learning is very common and seems to work well in this setting. Understanding that this is not common in Argentina, she could have given him the option of soliciting audience participation and then informed the audience of his preference.

When working with congregations or communities, it is very important to understand the degree to which they are hierarchical. If the hierarchy is ignored, serious problems in relationships may arise, for example, a culture's beliefs about hierarchy influence who has status and why. Most hierarchical cultures adhere to some degree to *ascribed status* or status given to one by virtue of position in life.[2] This would include gender, age, caste, tribe, family, wealth and so on. Egalitarian cultures more typically base status on achievement, referred to as *achieved status*.[3]

Let's say you were looking for someone from a culture community to help you in planning an event. If you come from an egalitarian culture, you would probably look for someone who seemed to have the skills or interest to participate. If you come from a hierarchical culture, most likely you would look for someone who had ascribed status in the community, regardless of skill or interest. What happens in the United States when someone is working with a hierarchical culture? Often the wrong leaders are enlisted and a project that would have otherwise succeeded is now doomed to fail. The opposite is also true; a project with many problems can be saved if the culturally correct person is participating. If a person from a hierarchical culture is charged with selecting a leader, the same mistake can be made by selecting the person believed to have the ascribed status rather than one with the achieved status.

Recently a Christian ministry sponsored an ecumenical Christian women's retreat. After the success of the first retreat, they decided to make it an annual event. In order to get more local participation they formed a committee of local Christian women. Since they did not have many contacts with churches of other cultures, they asked other Anglos about ethnic persons whom they would recommend to be on this steering committee. With these recommendations, they invited about half a dozen women to be on the committee. All of the women were talented and able to do what was needed to assist in the preparation and planning of the retreat. The Mexican and Korean women agreed to serve. Three African American women, all from the same church, also agreed to be on the committee. Only the Japanese woman declined to serve, explaining she did not think she was the right person for the honor. The ministry thought they had put together a great multicultural planning team. But there was a problem.

Egalitarian and hierarchical cultures view leadership and status very differently.

All these women had been selected by cultural outsiders. The Mexican woman agreed to serve because she was afraid that if she declined no other Hispanic would be on the committee. She was embarrassed to tell the other women in her church that she had been asked to serve on the committee. Because the culturally appropriate person had not been approached, she needed to keep her involvement a secret so that it would not bring shame to the other woman or to the ministry. Her effectiveness at being able to promote the event was greatly diminished. It was the same for the Korean woman. The Japanese woman declined for the same reason, yet her fear was also of bringing shame on herself by agreeing to something that she knew would not be right unless the pastor approved and requested it.

The only women who were comfortable with the responsibility were the African American women. The explanation is simple if you understand the importance of ascribed status. The first African American woman asked was a pastor's wife. She agreed and selected two other women from her congregation. These women were functioning in a culturally appropriate way. The pastor's wife was the one with ascribed status and she knew which women could do what the committee needed. With her inclusion, they were free to participate and use the gifts they had. In the case of the other women, their ability to contribute all that they could was greatly reduced because they knew that they were violating a cultural standard.

Uncertainty Avoidance

Another aspect of the authority lens is uncertainty avoidance.[4] Although this may be a new term to you, it will not be a new concept. We are familiar with people who have varying degrees of comfort dealing with uncertainty and ambiguity. While we recognize these personal differences, we may not be aware that there are cultural preferences in this area as well.

Some cultures have *high uncertainty avoidance*. This means that as a whole the people of that culture are uncomfortable with ambiguous situations. As you might have already guessed, these cultures are more hierarchical and formal, thus avoiding the uncertainty that comes with a less structured environment.

Other cultures have *low uncertainty avoidance* and are comfortable in settings where things are ambiguous. Between these two extremes are many, many cultures. For our purposes, however, we will refer to those who fall on either side of the mid-line as either high or low.

This aspect of culture has a tremendous impact on the type of settings and situations conducive for multicultural participants. When I first began to do crosscultural consultations, I began to meet with pastors from various Asian countries. I had no agenda for the meetings except to create a forum whereby we could fellowship, pray or plan activities that would meet the needs they identified. We held the meetings at the building where I worked, which I knew some of them considered to be a "headquarters." In order to minimize that impression and the role of chair I thought they would assume for me, I worked to create a very casual atmosphere. I openly stated that I was not in charge and that I wanted everyone to share their ideas and my role would be to try to help make happen whatever the group wanted. I soon became frustrated, as did they. There was a great deal of discussion but no decisions. My doing culture wanted results. Unfortunately it took years for me to understand what was actually going on in our meetings. Without knowing it, I had created an environment that was very uncomfortable and disorienting for the participants. The informal atmosphere that I thought would help everyone feel comfortable had done just the opposite. The uncertainty of the setting was hindering the group's ability to know how to make decisions and assign responsibilities.

If I had understood the impact of uncertainty avoidance, I would have been able to make the meeting environment comfortable for the pastors' culture and not mine. By providing a clear picture of what I expected, empowering the ascribed status leaders and establishing what other groups had done in similar situations, I could have alleviated some of the uncertainty that hindered our desired outcome.

Cultures respond differently to the presence of ambiguity and uncertainty. Understanding other cultures' comfort levels will strengthen your multicultural connections.

Power Distance

Another factor in the authority lens is power distance.[5] "Power distance" refers to the comfort one has with unequal distribution of power. Having a large power distance means that you are comfortable with being separated from the source of power that has a direct impact on your life, or having large distances between you and the ones over which you have power. Stated another way, unequal distribution of power would not be a concern. For example, if your culture is a large power distance culture, having an authority (supervisor, politician and so on) tell you what to do with no opportunity for input may not be troublesome for you.

If your culture is a small power distance culture, however, this sort of situation may be virtually intolerable. "Small power distance" refers to a low tolerance for unequal distribution of power and great discomfort when there is little access to power.

In the previous illustration of the pastor's meeting, power distance was also a factor. I was very uncomfortable with the perception they had that I was the boss. I knew when I was referred to that way, it was meant as a compliment, but I was still uneasy with it. I wanted no power distance between us. The more I tried to downplay my role (seen as power), the more uncomfortable they became. The pastors had no problem with my taking a leadership role and, in fact, had I been willing to be more comfortable in that role, our relationships would have progressed more rapidly. I was creating an ambiguous, uncertain environment by trying to equalize the power.

Power distance can also be a factor in a relationship even when one or both parties are unaware that the issue of power is present. Persons who have lived life with a sense of personal power tend to minimize its effect on relationships. On the other hand, if one has grown up with the realization that he or she has little power, then power is a recognizable and formidable factor in many relationships. This could be played out in the following way.

Two coworkers are assigned to a project. As they begin to discuss how they will distribute the work, the Panamanian employee participates in the listing of tasks but takes no initiative to choose which tasks she will do. The U.S.-born Anglo almost immediately begins to select the tasks that she most enjoys. Her assumption is that if her coworker had preferences, she would speak up. The Anglo employee sees nothing in the interaction related to power because she believes that she and her partner are equal. In Panamanian culture, however, large power distance is accepted and normative. She may assume the position of less power even if her assumption is the only factor making it a reality. For these two coworkers to function well together both will need to understand the cultural lenses through which they view authority.

Many factors can determine whether a person assumes he/she or another has the power in a given situation. In the preceding illustration the Panamanian believed she was in a less powerful position than her coworker. This could have been based on tenure, education, position in the company, English skills and so on. In other situations her belief may be that she is in the more powerful position, and the encounter would look very different. It is important to note that among persons with a large power distance, who has the most power will be a factor in the relationship.

When very small power distance is tolerated, there is great opportunity for misunderstandings and misattributions to take place. This is especially true in a multicultural setting. Someone taking charge can be viewed as trying to create a greater power distance and people may react to that rather than to the leadership style or the direction the leader is going. Many times it is viewed by these cultures as control and efforts will be made to keep the power distance small, which can be seen as resistance. While the dominant U.S. culture has a small power distance, some minority cultures, such as Native American and African American, within the United States have even smaller power distances.

Issues of power distance are often hard to determine, but you can learn to identify them with experience and cultural knowledge.

Connecting

1. Refer to chapter two. Which of the questions reflect issues of authority? How did you respond? How do you fit within your cultural norms? Are you more or less egalitarian than your culture as a whole? If so, what has influenced you to be different?

2. Do you think the culture of Jesus' day was hierarchical or egalitarian? What New Testament stories lead you to that conclusion?

3. Name three idioms that you think reflect your culture's belief about authority.

4. Think about the settings in which you work or socialize with persons of other cultures. Do you differ in your cultural beliefs about authority? How

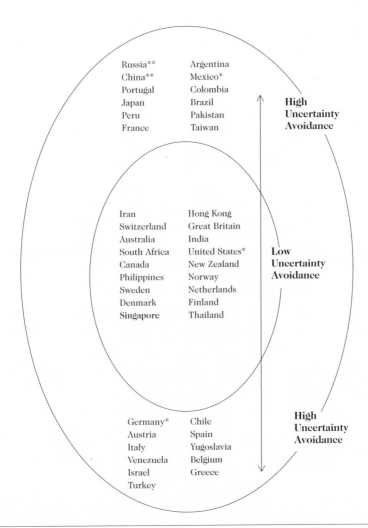

Figure 5.2. The uncertainty avoidance lens. Geert Hofstede, *Culture's Consequences* (Beverly Hills, Calif.: Sage, 1980), p. 315.

Original terms are strong (high) uncertainty avoidance and weak uncertainty avoidance.
*These country categories changed in the research conducted by Denise Rotondo Fernandez, Dawn S. Carlson, Lee P. Stepina, and Joel D. Nicholson in "Hofstede's Country Classification 25 Years Later," *The Journal of Social Psychology* 137, no. 1 (1997): 43.
**These countries were added in more recent research.

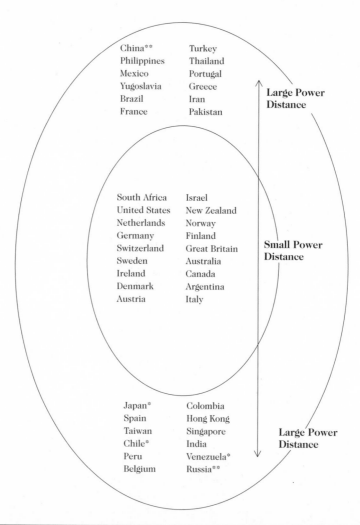

Figure 5.3. The power distance lens. Geert Hofstede, *Culture's Consequences* (Beverly Hills, Calif.: Sage, 1980), p. 315.

This data is based on workplace values.

*These country categories changed in research from Denise Rotondo Fernandez, Dawn S. Carlson, Lee P. Stepina, and Joel D. Nicholson in "Hofstede's Country Classification 25 Years Later," *Journal of Social Psychology* 137, no. 1 (1997): 43.

**These countries were added in more recent research.

is that reflected in your interactions?

5. How will this cultural difference impact the approach you take in sharing the gospel?

6. How will the issue of uncertainty avoidance impact the speed of friendship development?

7. Referring to figures 5.2 and 5.3, locate the countries that appear on both the High Uncertainty Avoidance list and the Large Power Distance list. These culture groups will be the most hierarchical.

8. Referring to figures 5.2 and 5.3, locate the countries that appear on both the Low Uncertainty Avoidance and Small Power Distance lists. These culture groups will be the most egalitarian.

6

Who Am I?
The Source of Identity

*"If we could stop assuming that other people are like us—if we could begin to believe
that we don't necessarily understand how foreigners are thinking
and that they don't always understand how we are thinking—then we would be
well on our way to avoiding cultural misunderstandings
and all the problems they give rise to."*
CRAIG STORTI

Understanding our own culture and those of others is only helpful if we apply what we learn to our relationships. The relationship
lens gives a focus to that dimension of culture. The relationship
lens can also be referred to as the identity dimension because these
beliefs not only form the basis for relationships with others but also
the basis for how we view ourselves.

Collective cultures view themselves as part of a group, which
usually is their family, tribe or community. As a result people in
these cultures relate to persons not only as unique individuals but
as part of a greater whole. Korean culture is a good example of a collective culture. Many Korean communities in the United States are
thriving, in part, because of their strong commitments to family
and each other. Their motto might be "one for all and all for one."[1]

Individualistic cultures see each person as an individual, separate from family or community. As a result people relate to each other on a one-on-one basis. Low context cultures such as the United States tend to be individualistic. The motto here might be "every person for him/herself."[2] The lens for the relationship dimension of culture is illustrated in figure 6.1.

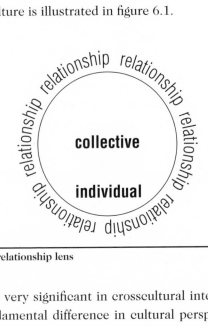

Figure 6.1. The relationship lens

This lens is very significant in crosscultural interactions. It represents a fundamental difference in cultural perspectives that impacts all relationships at some level and defines a major portion of one's identity.

I encountered this relational dimension my first year as a crosscultural church starter. One of our large Anglo churches was working to start a Cambodian church, and the Cambodian congregation was meeting temporarily in the educational wing of the church facility. One day I received a call from a very agitated children's minister. Her frustration level was high and she bluntly stated that she did not think her church should continue to try to help this Cambodian church. Her reason seemed sound—they were not Christians. She had formed this conclusion out of a series of events related to the supplies in the classrooms shared by the two churches.

"You see," she told me, "they keep stealing our supplies, even after we have clearly posted signs stating that these supplies are specifically for our church's children." I must admit I was surprised to learn of this obvious breach of ethics, but asked her to postpone action until I talked with the Cambodian pastor. I was concerned about how to do this in a way that would not embarrass him. Ultimately I was the one embarrassed, for this humble pastor taught me a lesson about collectivism and the church that I have never forgotten.

When I asked the pastor about the supplies, he began to express his gratitude toward God. He thanked God over and over for providing such a wonderful place for their congregation to meet and worship. He had felt so welcomed; this Anglo church had become his family. The more he talked, the more I understood. Neither he nor his teachers saw a distinction in what was the Anglo church's supplies and what was available for them to use. It was all bought with God's money and for God's church. They were a part of the whole church. It had never occurred to him that the Anglo congregation would view it any differently.

The conflict was cultural rather than ethical. It was our individualistic perspective that allowed us to feel ownership of even that which we had given to God. It was the Cambodians' collective perspective that assured them that what belonged to the church belonged to the whole church, not just one part of the church. With this new understanding, the children's minister and I designed a system that would allow the teachers to "own" their materials but also share with their fellow congregation.

Recognizing whether a person views life from an individualistic or collective perspective is critical in building meaningful relationships.

When life and relationships are viewed from a collective perspective, the issue of "face" or honor becomes extremely important. For collective cultures, the fear of "losing face," feeling shame or losing honor seems almost innate, as natural as breathing and as devastating as not breathing. It is a guiding force behind most interactions, or at the very least, the principle on which decisions are made as to what is appropriate behavior.

It is hard to find an equivalent in U.S. culture for this phenomenon. In most of the world it is much deeper and its consequences are more far-reaching than the English expression conveys. To lose face is to bring shame either on oneself or on one's family (or group to which one belongs). If one is not familiar with how this happens, one can cause another person to lose face or lose face oneself without even knowing it. Frequent causes of losing face are listed below, but keep in mind that in every culture there are unique ways in which loss of face or honor may occur. Loss of face can be caused by

☐ dishonoring oneself by not living up to certain goals

☐ actions of a family member

☐ not fulfilling another's expectations

☐ causing a person (or minority) to be out of unity with the group (or majority)

☐ suggesting that one is responsible for a problem or a difficulty

☐ losing in a real or perceived competition[3]

Losing face may be the hidden barrier to crosscultural relationships. The following stories from *Worldwide Business Practices* show the importance of face in other countries. For those of us in the United States who work with people whose culture is very close to the culture of their country of origin, understanding this dynamic is equally essential.

> Some time ago I was negotiating with about four Malaysians, and I had a couple of American associates with me. We were in the middle of technical negotiations. One of the Malaysians got confused between metric and U.S. measurements on a certain item. That immediately screwed up all the prices and specs. The normal way I would do it in the States is to correct that person and move along. You can't do that in Malaysia. Instead, I called a tea break. I took that gentleman aside and explained to him that because of our poor description of the item, it was not clear, and therefore he had

misinterpreted it. We went then back into the room and I apolo-
gized to the other side for the confusion. The negotiations continued along and face was saved.

When you schedule meetings with Malaysians, you should expect that they are going to be late. . . .They are not sending you a
message that you are not important. The higher ranking the Malaysian person is, the more likely he or she is going to be late. It is
part of giving face and showing respect to take it with a smile and
not to expect an apology. Westerners, however, are expected to be
on time. If we are late, we are sending the message that we do not
respect [them].[4]

In almost all of my work the understanding of face is critical and
sets up many situations that appear to put me in the middle, in a
no-win position. As an employee of my organization I am expected
to deal with matters straight on, quickly discerning a situation and
solving it. Yet my understanding of culture dictates that indirectness will actually be my best method of achieving what I hope will
be our common goals. Many times my need for expediency and results battles with my cultural knowledge. Experience has taught
me, however, that it is always best to keep the concern for my face
and theirs foremost in my mind as we communicate. To ignore this
not only compounds the problem, but makes reaching a solution
exponentially harder.

The preservation of face is of great importance, especially with
new friendships. Learning the art of being indirect will be a valuable
skill. Being indirect in confronting issues is done to save face. Even
the specific words chosen need to be soft and indirect, always pro-
tecting the other person's sense of honor or face. Many people who
are unaware of the issue of face misattribute to this behavior a desire to avoid taking responsibility or being too concerned about
their own pride. However, when there is an understanding of the
significance of face and the need for it to be safeguarded, indirectness becomes an effective tool to accomplish that goal and not an
escape from responsibility.

Suggestions to Avoid Losing Face or Causing Another to Lose Face

Do not ask questions that will force the other person to admit a mistake, namely, "Did you forget to bring in the mail?" or "I brought the work by on Tuesday, and you said that you would be finished by today. Why aren't you done?" Instead, approach the matter like this, "I cannot find the mail, would you help me?" "I know you have not had much time since Tuesday, but when do you think I will be able to pick up the finished work?" These may seem like questions designed to help the other person avoid admitting responsibility, and in part, that is right. They are designed to avoid having to admit failure or error. The understanding of responsibility is culturally defined. For individualistic cultures it is important that each individual accept and admit responsibility for actions or lack of actions. However, in collective cultures this is not a priority. The sense of being a part of the group, in harmony, "one for all and all for one" is more important. Responsibility is felt deeply. There is no need to make the person admit it, but there is a need to allow the person to save face in order to then have the freedom to make it right.

Listen for the answer to yes/no questions. If the answer to a yes/no question is no, the answer may not be stated. Instead, you may hear, "not yet," "I don't think so" or even "that's fine." Being able to understand an indirect no is important.

Pay attention to cultural etiquette. Obviously there will be many rules of etiquette that you will not know, but if a matter of protocol has been shared with you, do not ignore it because you think it is silly or uncomfortable. When you do this you lose face in their eyes. It is as if you are asserting that you and your ways are superior to theirs. For example, if I go to visit my Lao friends I know that I should take my shoes off at the doorway. If I go on in wearing my shoes, they will not say anything to me about it, but I may have lost face in their eyes.

Be complimentary. Many cultures concerned with face are very effusive in their compliments and praise. It is good to reciprocate, but it is also important to know that when you receive such high praise it may only be given to you as a cultural courtesy. You will know their real opinion by their actions more so than by their words.

Show respect. This includes using titles and formality if that is their custom. It may be hard to know the specific acts that convey respect to each culture that you meet. However, by displaying an attitude of admiration and personal humility, even if you don't know all the specifics, you will demonstrate your respect.

Make an effort to understand their positions on context, authority, activity, relationships and time (discussed in the next chapter). By understanding these you will be more sensitive to issues that would cause loss of face. For example, if I know that my friend is from a being culture, I will not expect results to be reported in facts and figures. Therefore, I will not cause her to lose face by asking for that information without preparing her for it first.

Do not set up competitions. This would include trying to motivate by competition, namely, "All the other departments are adding new services, don't you want to be as innovative as they are?" This approach can cause one of two problems. The person can lose face and thus be too ashamed to try anything new for fear of further failure or not meeting expectations, or the person can become less motivated because he knows the other departments are doing so well that the pressure is off them to perform. Remember that most collective cultures are the ones concerned about face. They do not view themselves in isolation but as part of the group. So, if all the other departments are doing well, they are too because they are a part of that whole.

Do not ask questions implying that the other is in need. It is common in individualistic cultures to ask, "What do you need?" or "How can I help you?" However, one might get better results if the questions were phrased, "How can we partner together on this?" or "What do you think will be necessary?" Even these slight modifications can make a big difference in how one is perceived. Implying one is in need is a subtle way of shaming in some more collective cultures. As I was discussing this with an African American friend of mine, she confirmed how important this is. She said, "I do not like it when someone from another culture or race assumes things about me. I hear them say 'What do you need?' and I think, *What makes you think I need anything?* It makes me feel like they think they are better than me. It is embarrassing to me to think that is what people assume about me. I always wonder if that assumption is based on a stereotype of my race."

Now for those who are culturally attuned to issues of face, you may benefit from learning the language and skills of polite directness. The U.S. dominant culture is very direct. Understanding this and what it means will be an asset in building relationships with your individualistic neighbors. Remember the traits of low context, doing, egalitarian cultures. Life is compartmentalized and result oriented. Add to that a belief in the equality of all and you have a cluster of characteristics that lead to a more direct form of communication. It may seem like this is a more harsh and impolite way in which to relate to your fellow humans, but for those persons who are culturally accustomed it works very well. You can feel safe in assuming that a direct question is not asked in order to cause you to lose face. If answered directly, the conversation will move on and no other meaning will be ascribed to it. In fact, the likelihood of something being read into an answer is much greater with an indirect answer.

For example, if I ask my Korean friend if he has found out if the store will be opened on Sunday and he replies, "I don't think so," I am likely to be confused. My thought would be "Doesn't he know if he found out or not?" Only after understanding the importance of saving face and indirectness would I be able to hear that answer as "no."

One technique used by some people in the United States is to preface a direct comment or question with "May I be blunt?" or "I am going to speak frankly" or "I hope it is okay if I am direct." By doing this they hope to prepare the person for the directness of the comment, to obtain a loose form of consent and to acknowledge that it might sound blunt. I would encourage you to observe conversations between U.S. Americans. The way in which directness is approached varies regionally and between different microcultures. For example, New Yorkers may tend to be more direct in their conversations than rural Southerners.

There seems to be no research on what would be a U.S. cultural value equivalent to face. I have informally interviewed those living here from other cultures and have found several recurring guesses as to what it might be. Most observe that at its deepest level the U.S. dominant culture values self-reliance, autonomy and personal rights. Immigrants and those from the nondominant cultures of the United States suggest that understanding this provides great discernment into many interactions with persons of U.S. culture.

People from collective cultures find it hard to understand why U.S. Americans insist on their "fair share" even at the risk of embarrassing someone else or even when they compete within a family. Nor do they understand when one insists on stating a personal opinion even when it is out of harmony with the group. U.S. Americans find this commendable, an assertion of their autonomy and individualism, but collective cultures find it rude and immature.

It is probably this dichotomy of fears—losing face and losing personal rights—that sets up the other cultural differences observed in the relationship lens. It is easy to see how collective cultures that favor interdependence and cooperation would fear losing face, and individualistic cultures that favor independence and competition would fear losing autonomy.

Mai Ling and Susan are both starting first grade today. Both their families are excited about this milestone and each family has advice on this momentous occasion. Mai Ling's family tells her to be a good student, listen to her teacher, do what she says and not to call attention to herself. In addition, Mai Ling should be a good friend to her classmates, help them if needed and be willing to share whatever she has.

Susan's family too, wants to pass on words of wisdom to help Susan adjust positively to this new phase of her life. Susan is told to work hard, ask questions if she doesn't understand and keep up with her supplies, which have all been marked with her name. She must not let anyone pick on her, but if they do she should be sure to tell her teacher.

While these scenarios will vary from family to family, you can see how culture shapes a person's perspective, even the first day of school. Think about the impact of a lifetime of shaping.

Our identity as an individual or as a part of a group and our fear of losing "face" or losing autonomy are foundational to how we view responsibility, competition and independence.

Connecting

1. Refer to the questions in chapter two. Which questions reflect issues discussed in this chapter—collectivism, individualism, competition, cooperation, independence and interdependence?

2. What values do these idioms/expressions teach?

☐ The squeaky wheel gets the grease.

☐ Just looking out for number one.

☐ Self-made man

☐ My way or the highway

☐ Every man for himself

☐ He pulled himself up by his own bootstraps.

Write down idioms you know that express opposite values. Check with a person of a collective culture, if you cannot think of any.

3. Write down the emotion that each of the following words evokes. For example one may respond to "privacy" by feeling "lonely" or feeling "safe."

Privacy	Group	Family
Relationships	Alone	Independent
Self-sufficient	Dependent	Involved

Do you see your cultural values expressed in your emotional responses to these words?

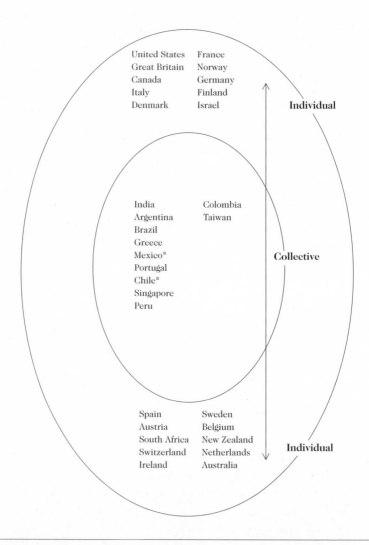

Figure 6.2. The collective/individual lens. Geert Hofstede, *Culture's Consequences* (Beverly Hills, Calif.: Sage, 1980), p. 315.

This data is based on workplace values.
*These country categories changed in research from Denise Rotondo Fernandez, Dawn S. Carlson, Lee P. Stepina, and Joel D. Nicholson in "Hofstede's Country Classification 25 Years Later," *Journal of Social Psychology* 137, no. 1 (1997): 43.

4. Look at the passage in Matthew 25:31-46. What cultural perspective does Jesus reflect? What implication does this have for us as Christians? Think of other passages; do they reflect collectivism or individualism? Look at Acts 16:25-34. What cultural factors are evident in this account?

5. Think of your culture's history. What factors have led you to hold the cultural views on individualism or collectivism that you do? Do you personally differ from your culture as a whole? What are the factors that have influenced you to be different?

7

When Do We Start?
Our Sense of Time

"Timing is everything." "Time is money." "My time is your time." "It's about time."
"Time is running out." "Time management is essential."
"My most valuable possession is time." "Wasting time."
COMMON EXPRESSIONS IN THE UNITED STATES

Usually the first cultural difference I hear people talk about is the difference in dealing with time. Have you ever heard someone comment, "They are on 'Latin time'"? (You can change the word *Latin* for many other countries or culture groups.) Unfortunately, to most U.S. Americans there is a pejorative sound to the phrase. Many in the United States believe that punctuality is a virtue and have never thought about other ways of being on time, other than noting the "clock" time.

The temporal lens of culture deals with both the twenty-four-hours-in-a-day-time as well as the nature of time. Some cultures, primarily the United States, Canada and Western European countries, view time as *limited and evolving*.[1] Time is seen as a possession, a resource to be used wisely. The big picture of time is that it is evolving, moving along in a line from point A to point B to point C and so on throughout history.

Most of the rest of the world holds to different views of time, time as *abundant and historical*.[2] Those with this belief system may find the "clock watchers" too rigid and not focused on the important aspects of life. The clock watchers, however, find it inconceivable that any group of people could actually function and get anything done without attention being paid to what they consider real time.

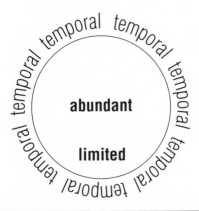

Figure 7.1. The lens of time

Once when I was teaching on this subject, a U.S. native came to me afterwards and told me that while living in Kenya he had learned an important lesson about the differences in time perspective. He plainly admitted that his first six months in the country were frustrating for him because nothing ever started on time and so much time was wasted waiting on people to arrive. He had tried some things he had heard others do, such as telling people an earlier time so if they were an hour late it would be the time he had planned to start anyway. But the longer he lived in Kenya and the more he observed Kenyan relationships, the more he understood what was actually happening. The Kenyans were not always running late, being irresponsible or not caring about an event, but rather they ran on a different timetable. They started on time no matter what a clock said, because they started when all the people who needed to be there were there.

This is a perfect example of the view that time is abundant and just because a person changes his/her geographical location, it doesn't mean that cultural values have been changed. There are many cultures, Kenyan and others, in the United States that share this same perspective on time. Time is seen from many perspectives, not just the movement of the sun. Each culture deals with the temporal dimension of life in a way that best suits its environment and other important aspects of its culture. It is easy to see why doing cultures would see time as a possession and a means to achieve an end (results) and why a being culture, which values relationships and quality of life, would be more concerned about starting when everyone was there.

When establishing relationships it is important to remember that some cultures see time from a historical perspective, a history of interactions and events. It is this history that forms one of the most binding elements of a relationship.

One year I was asked to attend a meeting between two congregations, a sponsor church (Anglo, middle-class) and a new church (Nigerian) with whom the Anglos were sharing their facilities. The two churches were at an impasse over issues related to the Nigerian church's pastor. Relationships and trust between the leaders of the two churches had been dismantled in the previous weeks, and this was to be their last effort at a peaceful separation. Understanding the importance of history for the Nigerian congregation, I began to reference events in which I had participated together with them. As we began to recall these pleasant times, their tension began to decrease. The fact that we had shared significant life events and that I remembered and valued them created an opening for me to be heard and be a legitimate participant in the dialogue.

While this new congregation began to relax, I noticed the tension mounting among the leadership in the Anglo church. I had been aware of the need to be sensitive to the abundant (take as much time as you need to work the situation out) and the historical importance of time for the Nigerians. I had, however, forgotten that the Anglo church would become impatient with what seemed to them to be small talk that wasted time. The inability of the two churches' leaders to understand time from the other's perspective prohibited each church from receiving what they wanted, a restoration of the relationship. Instead communication broke down and the two churches severed their relationship.

This lack of understanding in the temporal lens has also created some of the misattributions that contribute to racial tensions between Anglo and African American communities. How many times has someone who is not African American commented on their frustration that African Americans won't "just get over the past." "Sure," they admit, "bad things were done to slaves, but it is time to get over it." To an African American it is not that simple. Time is historical and the past is part of the present and cannot be ignored or just gotten over. In the linear view of time one moves from point A to point B and life goes on leaving the past behind. In the historical view of time one's history is always present in the now.

This difference in viewing time can even color perceptions of the other group's spiritual values. When I was in seminary I had a good friend from Egypt. She was a seminary student as well, and in between work, study, church and classes we tried to spend time together. One day at her apartment she made a startling announcement to me. She said quite definitively, "You know Americans are just too busy to be Christians." As you can imagine, I was surprised to hear her say that, so I asked her to explain what she meant.

She replied, "Americans, even those who call themselves Christians, are always having to do something or go somewhere. They say that they care about you, but they never just stop by to visit. When they call you it is just for a few minutes and it is usually because they need to get some information from you and not to see how you are. They talk about serving God and loving people, but I don't see how they can when they are so busy and have so much to do. Do they think that God wants them to live like that? I don't think they care what God wants. They have their schedules and that is their god. How can a real Christian survive here?"

I knew that most of this was directed at me, although she did not want to accuse me directly. I had not realized what a huge difference we had in the perception of time. While I had thought I was being very generous in the time we were spending together, she had seen that it was time I scheduled and when that time was up I moved on. The kind of time with Christian friends she had experienced in Egypt was not happening in the United States and her conclusion was that we were not real Christians. This conclusion was a misattribution, but it illustrates the difference in viewing time as either a limited resource to be managed or as an abundant gift to be used freely without constraint.

In ministry this time difference is most contentious in the sharing of facilities or the starting/ending of events. Many misattributions occur around this one issue. The limited-time group thinks that the abundant-time group is inconsiderate or disrespectful, while the abundant-time group perceives the limited-time group as unfeeling, rigid and without Christian priorities. The truth is that neither approach is right or wrong. Both approaches are appropriate within their own cultural settings. But what do we do when we face this cultural time difference within the United States? By whose rules will we live?

It is my opinion that there are workable solutions. First, it takes valuing the other's frame of reference and being committed to try to meet the felt needs of both cultures. The following are some options that have been tried by those with a limited time perspective, but have not been found helpful in building relationships:

☐ Tell a group an earlier time so that when they are late they may actually be on time.

☐ Make misattributions about what this difference means, such as "They must not care about this event, they are irresponsible, and so on."

☐ Always start by the clock and thereby meet without the other culture present.

☐ Call attention to someone's lateness in order to embarrass them into being "on time" the next time.

☐ Undertake drastic measures such as locking doors, turning off lights and so on in order to force a group to leave.

Instead, read the following and see if you can determine the steps taken to come to a successful solution and also to help forge a stronger relationship and better communication.

One year I was assigned the responsibility of enlisting several ethnic churches to participate in a program at our annual convention. It was very important to my supervisors that we be prompt. My job was to make sure that everyone I had enlisted was on time. Being new at my job I was not certain how to ensure that this would happen, short of spending the day personally picking up all forty people (and even that would be no guarantee). I decided to visit with each pastor and explain how important it was to me personally and to our organization that we follow a tight schedule. I also explained that the program was dependent on their participation in order for the audience to know of their tremendous contribution to our work. After that I asked if there was anything that we could do to assist them to be there at the appointed time. Simple ideas, such as assigning people to specific cars ahead of time, centralized childcare and so on, were discussed and implemented.

Understanding other cultures' "clocks" will promote better relationships.

The night of the program everyone was there on time, some even early. I learned a valuable lesson. When I am honest, explain why the time schedule is important and recognize that my culture's way of telling time is different from theirs but not better, I have never had a disappointment with someone not being "on time." I do not follow this in every situation because it is not always so important to be on a rigid schedule. While other approaches may work in a given situation, a positive solution can be obtained through discussion, and the relationship can be built.

Connecting

1. What does being late mean in your culture?

2. What misattributions have you made about someone else's lateness?

3. How did Jesus view time? What passages can you think of where time is an issue? In what context is it an issue?

4. What is your culture's view of time? How do you see that view in relation to other dimensions of your culture?

5. How did you learn your perspective on time?

6. Have you/are you living in a culture with a different perspective of time than yours? How did you/are you adapting? How has that adjustment felt?

8

What's Really Real?
Differences in Worldview

*"The world is divided not so much by geographic boundaries
as by religious and cultural traditions,
by people's most deeply held beliefs—by worldviews."*
CHARLES COLSON

To some degree, all relationships reflect the participants' understanding of reality—their worldview. In a crosscultural relationship the difference between realities can be staggering.

In this chapter we will briefly explore three worldview approaches and then look at how worldview impacts our understanding of reality. This will in no means be a thorough study of worldviews. In fact, it will only serve to introduce the reader to the issue and emphasize the point that what one accepts as real is culturally based. It is a common mistake in crosscultural relationships to assume that we all see reality in the same way.

Worldview is extremely complex but necessary to understanding the heart of cultural differences. Our worldview is at the core of who we are. Think of the illustration of objective and subjective culture (the iceberg) in chapter two, and picture worldview as the foundation upon which the iceberg rests. It is the bedrock of subjective culture and the base upon which each culture's beliefs, values and customs are built.

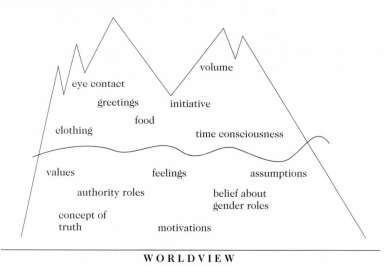

WORLDVIEW

Figure 8.1. Worldview is the foundation of culture

Worldview is the "culturally agreed upon perception of reality, in other words worldview bridges the gap between objective reality and a person's perception of it."[1]

Worldview reflects "how" a culture thinks. The "how" we think can create barriers in crosscultural relationships as much as the "what" we think. To know how best to communicate, one needs to know how a person thinks. Currently we think of the "how" from three perspectives—premodern, modern and postmodern.[2]

Woven into these worldviews are a multitude of variables. Table 8.1, based on information from Rex Miller and Brad Cecil, may help you understand these different approaches.[3]

Let's look at how these differences impact spiritual matters. People with different approaches can hold the same religious beliefs. In other words, a person can be a Christian, Deist, Buddhist, Muslim and so on, and be premodern, modern or postmodern in his/her manner of thinking. How people arrive at their faith beliefs, how they will communicate them to others and how the beliefs are applied to everyday life is determined by "how" they think, that is,

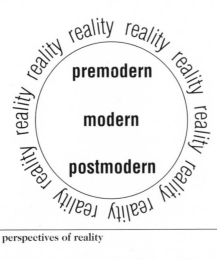

Figure 8.2. Three perspectives of reality

their worldview. Some worldviews lend themselves more easily to one faith system than another, for example, animism is more likely to be found in a premodern worldview.

Both premodern and postmodern thinkers accept spiritual realities more easily than modern thinkers. Premodern thinkers accept what appear to be inconsistencies and incongruities in what they believe. Postmodern and modern thinkers need verification but ac-

Table 8.1. Variables that comprise worldview

	Premodern	Modern	Postmodern
Truth	Subjective (tradition)	Objective	Subjective (experience)
Knowledge	Mystical (capricious)	Scientific	Mystical (understandable)
Perspective	Holistic	Dualistic, linear	Holistic
Evidence	Experiential (group then individual)	Empirical	Experiential (individual then group)

cept it in very different forms. Postmodern people want verification through experience, modern people through scientific study.

As you read the following story, think of the ways in which the fundamental differences in worldview are shaping this interaction.

Jackie and Bill are developing a relationship with Luc and Li. They have been drawn together because their third grade children have become best friends. Luc and his family are first generation immigrants from Vietnam. They have been in the United States for six years and during that time have developed good English communication skills. Jackie and Bill consciously work at bringing up spiritual matters with Luc and Li. They all seem to be in agreement about the importance of knowing Jesus, and Luc and Li have prayed to receive Jesus.

You can imagine their surprise when their daughter came home telling about the altar set up to Luc's ancestors with real food on it! They did not understand this custom nor did they know what to say to their daughter. After praying and talking with their minister, Jackie and Bill went to visit Luc and Li. They saw for themselves the altar and began asking questions about its meaning.

Luc explained the Vietnamese tradition of ancestor veneration. He believed it was important for him to pray to and honor his ancestors in order to secure their protection and blessing for himself and his family. In addition, Luc had a responsibility to honor his dead relatives so that they could be happy in their new lives. He explained that this tradition had been carried on in his family for hundreds of years.

Bill wanted to laugh. How could anyone believe such nonsense? But he refrained from commenting and began instead to ask questions about Luc's faith in Jesus. It soon became obvious that Luc saw no problem with believing in Jesus and venerating his ancestors.

Jackie began to talk to him and to Li, trying to explain how their ancestors had no power to effect their lives. She also emphasized that Luc had no ability to secure a happier life for people who were already dead. She went on to share how their faith in Jesus was all they needed. They could pray to him and he would help them. The ancestors were dead and there was nothing they could do for them now. This prompted Luc's question, "Does this mean that my ancestors are in hell?" Sadly Jackie told him that if they had not believed in Jesus they would not be with him in heaven when he died. Luc immediately said he would not believe in Jesus then because he could not be responsible for his parents and grandparents being in hell.

All efforts to persuade him that what he believed would have no bearing on the final destination of anyone but himself were futile. The visit came to an end and the two couples said a sad goodbye.

What happened in this encounter? Jackie and Bill are modern thinkers and, therefore, scientific, rational and analytical. They are evangelical Christians and want to share their faith in Christ with their friends. They have had good experiences with introducing others to Christ by simply sharing their testimony and Bible verses and answering the other person's questions. This is the approach they used with Luc and Li and they thought that their new friends had become believers in Christ, because they had prayed to "receive Christ."

Luc and Li are premodern thinkers and do not have to have everything add up or line up in a "logical" way. In fact they do not even think in terms of whether their thinking is "logical," because it is not analyzed in that way. They are very grateful for Jackie and Bill's friendship and are especially glad that their daughter has a good friend. The Jesus that Jackie and Bill talk about sounds wonderful and they have been excited to learn about him. Most of all they want to respect their new friends by not rejecting their beliefs. They have no problem adding Jesus to the other beliefs they have.

This interaction is fundamentally a difference in worldview. It is the clash of a worldview that is analytic; processes information in either/or (dualistic) categories and one that does not try to figure out the world through analysis, but draws conclusions from relationships, experiences and traditions. Jackie and Bill did not understand this, so they were confused when Jesus was just added to the other belief systems present in Luc and Li's life. On the other hand, Luc and Li did not understand that they had been asked to choose Jesus to the exclusion of their traditional way.

An understanding of their differences in worldview would have helped to avoid this situation. If Jackie and Bill had known that Luc and Li would want to add Jesus to their other religious beliefs and practices, then they could have addressed that issue in the beginning. They could have been particularly sensitive to their concerns. More important, they could have talked about Christian traditions and introduced them to other Vietnamese Christians who could have shared how they have come to believe in Jesus and how they were able to deal with their traditional, cultural beliefs. If this same scenario had still happened Jackie and Bill would have known to be patient, giving them time to reconsider the question when they had further teaching and experience as followers of Christ.

Different worldviews can be a barrier to good communication and relationships at a deeper level.

These three basic worldviews lead to belief systems too numerous to list. But as an example, table 8.2 represents a few that you may encounter in crosscultural relationships.

Now if you are one who believes that most illnesses are caused by germs/biology, then the usual treatment will be medication or surgery. If the medication does not bring about a cure, what is the conclusion? There could be one of several: it was not the right medication, it was not the right strength of medication, it was not the right diagnosis, or it was not the right doctor. The worldview, which dictates the basic cause—biology—is not questioned. It is the same with the other worldviews. When the remedy does not work, it does not mean to the adherent that the worldview is wrong, but only that some adjustment must be made (that is, go to a different doctor, try a new medicine and so on).[4]

Table 8.2. Sample of beliefs influenced by worldview

1. *What faith system do you believe in?*						
Judaism	Buddhism	Animism	New Age	Christianity	Naturalism	Folk religions

2. *What causes illness?*						
Evil spirits	Germs	Imbalance of energy	Soul left	A curse	Broken relationships	Bad luck

3. *What causes good things?*						
God (gods) favor you	Blessed because you did something good	Good karma	Fate	Good luck	Natural outcome of hard work	

4. *What causes hardships?*						
Punishment for wrong doing	Part of life to be expected	God trying to get one's attention	Fate	Don't exist unless you think they do	Natural outcome of one's lifestyle	

5. *What is the purpose of life?*						
Serve others	Make your next life better	Make your ancestors' lives better	Be self-ful-filled	Serve God, give God glory	No purpose other than pleasure	Repro-duce

Let's look at how this plays out by focusing on one of these categories in table 8.3.[5]

Table 8.3. The relationship of worldview, belief systems and behavior

Cause of Illness	Treatment
Evil spirits	Appease or rid yourself of the evil spirits
Biology/Germs	Medicine, surgery
Imbalance of energy	Balance energy (acupuncture, and so on)
A curse	Remove the curse
Broken relationships with people, nature or God (gods)	Restore relationships
Soul loss	Have the soul returned

The power of worldview is enormous because it sets the boundaries for what one understands as reality. Of all the cultural lenses this one may be the most important and the most difficult to understand. For illustration, let's continue with the example of the causes and treatments of illness. In the book *The Spirit Catches You and You Fall Down* the author describes the Hmong (a people group from northern Laos) worldview related to health.

> Most Hmong believe that the body contains a finite amount of blood that it is unable to replenish, so repeated blood sampling, especially from small children, may be fatal. When people are unconscious, their souls are at large, so anesthesia may lead to illness or death. If the body is cut or disfigured, or if it loses any of its parts, it will remain in a condition of perpetual imbalance and the damaged person not only will become frequently ill but may be physically incomplete during the next incarnation; so surgery is taboo.[6]

The Hmong worldview is premodern, and these specific Hmong beliefs related to the body, blood and afterlife are crucial pieces of information for anyone seeking to provide medical care to Hmong. These specific beliefs are important to know, but just as essential is the awareness that their worldview is premodern. Without this understanding it will be impossible to try to find ways to communicate what Western medicine believes to be normal medical treatment. Whenever you are communicating a message that requires deep personal understanding, such as matters of faith, healthcare and family relationships, the more you know and can explore the other person's worldview—what is their reality—the more successful you will be.

Each culture has specific beliefs based on its worldview perspective—how one thinks. From the how one thinks, belief systems are created and passed down from generation to generation with varying degrees of adaptation between generations. For real connections to be formed between people of different cultures, an awareness of each other's worldview and beliefs must be achieved. This does not mean that you agree with the other's worldview, but that you understand the boundaries of reality that the person has.

This is particularly true in relationships where you are sharing your faith. As was previously stated, all three approaches to "how" one thinks can be Christian, but there are some beliefs that grow out of that approach that are incompatible with Christian beliefs. For example, the belief that there are no absolutes in this world is incompatible with Christian teaching that God has absolutes. This creates a dilemma. While Christ died for all people and his message is for all nations (cultures, peoples), deciding what are mutually exclusive elements of the Christian faith is difficult and the answer has varied throughout history.

The first Jewish Christians were faced with this dilemma, as we can see in the book of Acts. Some of the Jewish leaders wanted the Gentile believers to be circumcised and follow the Jewish rituals and customs in order to be accepted as true believers (Acts 15:1-5). Ultimately they decided only to encourage them to "abstain from food sacrificed to idols, from blood, from meat of strangled animals and from sexual immorality" (Acts 15:29).

Others who have spread the gospel to different cultures have taught that once a person becomes a Christian, a rejection of previously held cultural traditions and an acceptance of the Western belief system and behaviors should follow. Evidence of this can be found by visiting Africa and Asia where Western style church buildings and worship format are common. This has led to a great misunderstanding about what it means to be a Christian. It also explains why Christianity is considered by many to be a "white man's religion" or a "Western religion." But is that accurate? What beliefs does a person need to have in order to be a Christian? What beliefs would be incompatible with those beliefs considered necessary to be a Christian? These are critical questions if one is to share the gospel with persons of other cultures. Not addressing them results in syncretism.

Syncretism—the blending of different or opposing religious/spiritual principles, beliefs and practices into one system of belief—is a threat to true Christianity. It allows for the blending of many beliefs and cultural practices into what may be called Christianity, but is not Christian in its fundamental beliefs. It is a serious problem in the church today and not just for the church in newly evangelized areas. Much of what is called Christian in the United States is really syncretism, a blending of U.S. cultural values and Christian teaching into a system that reflects more of who we are culturally than who God has called us to be as His followers. Thus many of our evangelistic efforts have required converts to adopt our cultural values and practices as well as Christian beliefs, the same issue the early church dealt with.

When the one sharing the gospel message cannot distinguish essential Christian truth from cultural values, it is easy to communicate one's culture as Christianity. This leaves no room for the new believer to discover through the Holy Spirit how God would have Christianity be expressed through that particular culture. It also perpetuates values that are cultural to the messenger and not universally Christian. It conveys that Christianity is locked into a cultural set of values and practices and all cultures that want to accept the good news of Jesus must leave their own culture behind and adopt that of the messenger.[7]

The Bible is our guide in how to deal with syncretism. The early church leaders in Acts 15 decided that when the conversion of people from another culture takes place, it is not the responsibility of the evangelizing group to require the new converts to adopt their culture. It is the Holy Spirit's task to convert the worldview of the new believer. In each culture the converted worldview may take on a different appearance because of cultural, geographical and physical uniqueness. Each culture has areas that are incompatible with Christian principles, including the culture of those who are evangelizing. It is difficult to discern what needs to change for another culture because one's own culture will likely get in the way. Medical anthropologist and psychiatrist, Arthur Kleinman, puts it this way, "If you can't see that your own culture has its own set of interests, emotions, and biases, how can you expect to deal successfully with someone else's culture?"[8] Together believers from different cultures can pray and study to discern where God is leading them to move beyond their human cultures and discover God's reality for their lives.

Connecting

1. What is your worldview?

2. What worldview (premodern, modern, postmodern) is reflected in the Bible? Look at some of Paul's writings. What were some of the boundaries of his reality? For example, did he believe the world was flat? Did he believe that germs caused illness and so on? Does this strengthen or weaken your view of inspiration?

3. How do you respond when you encounter someone whose worldview is different from that of yours? (You may want to think about the table with the different causes of illness and pretend you are dealing with someone who believes illness is caused and cured in a different way than you believe.)

4. How would/could someone begin to change your worldview? Has that ever happened?

5. What are some realities you accept that you know others do not? The following categories may help get you started.

☐ How is truth defined, experienced and shared?

☐ Who or what is in control?

☐ Are there absolutes? How do you know?

☐ Who can be trusted?

6. It is important to be able to determine what are essential to the faith and what are negotiable. This exercise from *The Other Side* contains items that Christians at one time considered important to the church. Mark each item as either essential or negotiable.

☐ Greet each other with a holy kiss.

☐ Do not go to court to settle issues between Christians.

☐ Do not eat meat in pagan ceremonies.

☐ Women in the church should be veiled when praying or speaking.

☐ Wash feet at the Lord's Supper (Eucharist).

☐ Lay hands at ordination.

- ☐ Sing without musical accompaniment.
- ☐ Abstain from eating blood.
- ☐ Abstain from fornication.
- ☐ Share the Lord's Supper (Eucharist) together.
- ☐ Use only real wine and unleavened bread for Eucharist meals.
- ☐ Use only grape juice for Eucharist meals.
- ☐ Anoint with oil for healing.
- ☐ Women should not teach men.
- ☐ Women should not wear braided hair, gold or pearls.
- ☐ Men should not have long hair.
- ☐ Do not drink wine at all.
- ☐ Slavery is permissible if you treat slaves well.
- ☐ Remain single.
- ☐ Seek the gift of tongues.
- ☐ Seek the gift of healing.
- ☐ Lift your hands when you pray.
- ☐ People who don't work don't eat.
- ☐ Have a private "devotional time" every day.
- ☐ Say "amen" at the end of prayers.
- ☐ Appoint elders and deacons in every congregation.
- ☐ Elect the church leaders.
- ☐ Confess sins to one another.
- ☐ Confess sins privately to God.
- ☐ Give at least ten percent of your income/goods/crops to God.
- ☐ Construct a building for worship.
- ☐ Confess Christ publicly by means of baptism.
- ☐ Be baptized by immersion.
- ☐ Be baptized as an adult.
- ☐ Be baptized as a child/infant.
- ☐ Do not be a polygamist.
- ☐ Do not divorce your spouse for any reason.
- ☐ Do not divorce your spouse except for adultery.

Reflect on the process that you used to distinguish the essential from the negotiable. What principle(s) governed your decision? Your principle(s) should account for every decision. Are some of the essential items more essential than others? Are there any items that have nothing to do explicitly with Scripture at all?[9]

9

How Do You Resolve Conflict?

"When two elephants fight, it's the grass that gets hurt."
AFRICAN PROVERB

Conflicts are inevitable in life, even for Christians. It is also true that no matter how much you know about working with other cultures, no matter how carefully you examine each cultural lens, a disagreement, conflict or miscommunication will occur. This chapter will deal with cultural factors that cause these problems. It will also explore how we can expand our strategies to resolve conflicts.

One of the greatest obstacles to resolving conflicts when they occur is our inability to think outside the parameters of conflict resolution we have learned. These learned methods are culturally based, so it follows that when we expand our relationships to include those from other cultures we must also expand our conflict resolution options.[1]

How do you know if the conflict has a cultural basis? This question has no easy answer. The root of conflicts can be deep within a relationship or can be on the surface or anywhere in between. Many times a conflict has more than one root cause. In a crosscultural relationship often at least some aspect of the problem is culturally based.

Common Causes of Crosscultural Conflict

Misattribution is the greatest cause of conflict and misunderstanding. As mentioned in the first chapter, misattribution is ascribing meaning or motive to behavior based on one's own culture. Because cultural behaviors and values are so diverse, it is easy to see how misattribution can create an environment where behaviors can be misunderstood.

Joe and Sung are coworkers at a local bank. Joe, an African American, is out-going and outspoken. He is often thought of as the life of the office because he brings a great deal of energy to any project. Sung, a Korean American, is a hard worker but very quiet. Joe often teases Sung, as he does the others in the office, about being so quiet and makes comments designed to provoke a response. The more Sung is passive and ignores Joe, the more Joe antagonizes him. Joe is convinced that Sung is prejudiced and that is why he will not make eye contact with him or engage in the office banter. He begins to tell others how superior Koreans think they are to African Americans. He believes Sung's behavior is racially motivated.

Sung on the other hand fears Joe is targeting him because he is an immigrant. He is humiliated when he hears Joe make fun of his accent. He knows he has done nothing wrong to Joe. He has acted toward him as he has everyone else, so all he knows to do is to ignore him and hope that he will someday stop bothering him.

This example may seem somewhat silly. Why would grown men think and behave in such a way? Yet, it is all too common. Misunderstandings like this happen all the time in the workplace, in the church and in daily transactions. What really happened? Joe was being himself and doing what he always did with his office workers. When Sung did not respond to Joe's attempts to include him as Joe thought he should, Joe assumed a reason based on his own cultural experiences. He could have been right; but in a crosscultural relationship, chances are he would not have been and in this case he definitely was not.

Sung's response had nothing to do with Joe being African American or feeling superior to him. Sung had responded to Joe as he would have to anyone. Joe's boisterous antics made him uncomfortable. When Sung tried to have a conversation with Joe, his teasing and joking caused Sung to disengage from the conversation. Sung believed that the teasing was a sign of Joe's contempt and disrespect for him, as it would have been if someone from his culture had been doing the same thing. Both were making misattributions that were escalating a conflict situation.

Other causes of conflict include information, expectations, values and behaviors.[2]

Information. It is easy for anyone to receive incorrect or unreliable information, but when this happens in a crosscultural situation, the ensuing problems can be more difficult to resolve. Many times our assumptions are the source of incorrect information. For example, José is late for a meeting and I believe that he is from a culture that is not as time conscious as mine. I assume that is why he is late, and jokingly refer to "Mexican time" as I attempt to explain why I am starting the meeting without him. Later when José comes in, I learn that his child was ill and the doctor was running late on her appointments, thus causing him to be late. Not only have I operated on misinformation, I have shared it with others and so perpetuated misinformation and a stereotype.

Incorrect information may also occur when one person assumes the other person knows the background or shares the similar cultural assumptions. It is obvious that this could be a greater risk when working crossculturally than when in a homogenous situation. Many times we give only partial information about a situation with the understanding that everyone knows what that means. Assuming that the other person knows or understands your assumption creates a large amount of unreliable information between cultures. You may be sending signals with additional information, but to someone not from your culture, these signals go unnoticed.

These situations can be as simple as a casual comment "Let's have lunch" that is never followed up with a specific invitation, or saying "Let's meet at lunch time," assuming that all cultures eat lunch and that lunch will be eaten at the same time. It can be more serious when assumptions are made about what the length of a lunch meeting should be, and so one party expects to be on their way in one hour and the other won't even be ready to get down to business until after the meal is finished. Other ways in which this happens is with body language. Many times we expect people to pick up on our body language as part of our true message, but since body language has very different meanings across cultures, this can be a very unreliable means of communication.

In addition, the differing cultural values of what is appropriate disclosure may hinder the communication of some information, especially that of a more personal nature. For instance, if my neighbor, who is of my culture, asks how I am doing one month after I have lost my job, I will probably tell her, "I am hanging in there, but money is getting pretty tight."

However if, in a similar scenario, she asked a neighbor from Japan, he would probably tell her that everything is OK. Unless my neighbor knew that it would be a loss of face to say that he was struggling financially, she might mistakenly believe that he was actually doing fine. While this same scenario could happen between persons of the same culture, it compounds the problem in crosscultural situations because of the expectations assumed by each person.

Conflicts can be avoided by checking to make sure you have correct and reliable information.

Expectations. Different expectations can also be a source of conflict because of misinformation or just a general difference in understanding of what is appropriate in a situation. In the previous situation with my neighbor, her belief that our Japanese friend was all right financially even while out of a job would prompt her to do nothing. However, our Japanese neighbor would expect her to know that he could not be doing well under the circumstances. He would probably be confused as to why she would want to embarrass him by asking such a personal question. He would be further confused because while she seemed to show some interest in his family and circumstance, she was now doing nothing to be of assistance.

I remember learning this lesson the hard way. Frequently I would learn of a foreign-born colleague's hardship via a mutual friend. I would pray for them and then would either write a note or go by to visit. I was surprised to discover that many of these families perceived me as uncaring, while at the same time my peers from my culture thought I was going "above and beyond" to demonstrate concern and genuine caring. For those of other cultures, I was not doing what they expected and hurt feelings resulted. Their expectation was that once I was made aware of the situation, I would take action to remedy it. In my culture to presume to take unsolicited action would be considered intrusive. Neither of us had any idea that we had such major differences in our expectations.

I have also experienced this in reverse. Once when I was very ill, a friend of mine from an African country called me. I told her that I was sick and she offered to come over and bring me some food. I readily declined, truly not wanting anyone to see me in such a condition, not wanting to expose her to whatever I had and really not wanting any food. In her culture, however, she could not conceive of knowing of a person's illness and doing nothing so she came bearing much nourishment for my ills. I am afraid that my reaction to seeing her at my door communicated that we certainly had very different expectations in that situation.

Understanding different cultural expectations can facilitate better communication and the avoidance of conflict.

Values. Differing values contribute to conflict situations as well. While we seldom think of prioritizing our values, we do have a hierarchy which governs our decisions and our behavior. In *Multicul-tural Management*, Elashmawi and Harris report their findings on the ranking of values by country. Table 9.1 lists the top five values for four countries.[3]

Table 9.1. Cultural values ranked by country

Japan	United States	Russia	France
Relationship	Equality	Family security	Self-reliance
Group harmony	Freedom	Freedom	Freedom
Family security	Openness	Self-reliance	Openness
Freedom	Self-reliance	Openness	Relationships
Cooperation	Cooperation	Material possessions	Time

These differing cultural values create tensions internally as well as externally. If my highest value is self-reliance and I am working with someone who does not highly value that, then my efforts to safeguard that priority may be misunderstood. The value placed on saving face is often dismissed by cultures that do not place as high a value on relationships and group harmony. It is the similarity in values within cultures that helps us understand each other's behavior without verbal explanation.

When cultural values differ, conflicts may occur. Learning to respect the priority a person places on a value helps you to avoid these conflicts.

Behavior. Differing behaviors are the most easily recognized cause of conflict. Let's look at one behavior pattern—speech. Speech patterns such as rhythm, inflection and voice are learned behaviors. Usually when a person learns a new language, the speech pattern from the original language is retained. This is why, for example, an English as a Second Language class may have six students from different countries learning English from the same person, but each student will have a unique speech pattern that will be more similar to someone from their homeland than to anyone else in the class.

Now let's say that you are from the southern United States and are working with a person who has emigrated from Nigeria. Their English will probably have a British quality and vocabulary, but may also be fast with the accents on different syllables. This may require some intense listening, which soon becomes frustrating or even annoying. Now the content of the message is mixed with your emotions. Conflicts and misunderstandings can arise from such a simple thing as this.

Sometimes there are preconceived impressions of a speech pattern that inhibit good communication from the start. The staccato pattern of Koreans sometimes is perceived as anger, while the tone of the British may appear arrogant. Even the more common African American, Hispanic and Anglo speech patterns, dialects, accents and word usage carry subtle meaning to the listener that influences the communication. Prejudice based on misattributions of speech patterns also exists in the United States. How often does Hollywood portray a character with a slow Southern drawl as dim-witted?

The issue of speech seems small and petty, hardly the stuff of major conflict, yet it provokes such a spontaneous reaction that ideas can be formed and impressions made without the listener even knowing what occurred to shape those impressions. Can you imagine then the impact of more obvious behaviors?

It is important to be aware of the effect of speech in conflicts because of another little-recognized fact. Duane Elmer points out that in many parts of the world people are more comfortable speaking in the passive voice.[4] This is especially true in conflict. To many in the United States the use of passive voice is seen as a way to avoid responsibility. In return, the constant use of active voice may create a barrier by sounding too self-important or too confrontational.

Imagine a conversation between Solomon, from Africa, and his supervisor, Frank, from the United States.

Frank: Why didn't you come to the meeting this morning?

Solomon: The bus left without me, so my feet had to bring me.

Frank: Don't blame it on the bus. You must not have been
                there on time.

Solomon: I am sorry you are so angry about the meeting. What
                would you like me to do?

Frank: I want you to take responsibility for your actions and
                get here on time next time.

From Frank's perspective Solomon was irresponsible by missing the bus, but even more so by not owning up to it. Solomon, on the other hand, recognized his responsibility and admitted it in the way he knew how. His use of passive voice exacerbated the already tense situation for both men. Now, imagine Frank understood that Solomon would prefer to speak in the passive voice and that it was not a means of escaping his responsibility.

Or what if Solomon knew that in English the active voice was most often used and its use would not mean a loss of face? Understanding the speech patterns of each culture and the priority of values would have prevented this incident into escalating into something bigger. Imagine the conversation like this.

Frank: I was disappointed you weren't at the meeting.

Solomon: The bus left without me, so my feet had to bring me.

Frank: It is important for all of us to be there, so I will expect
                you to be on time at the next meeting and to get the in-
                formation you missed this morning from a coworker.

Or like this:

Frank: Why didn't you come to the meeting this morning?

Solomon: I missed my bus so I had to walk.

Frank: You will probably get there earlier next time, walking
                had to have taken forever.

Solomon: I will. Thank you for understanding.

When either person changes their first statement, the whole encounter takes a different turn. The more we understand the cultural behaviors and expectations of others the more we can avoid conversations that create disharmony.

Misattribution is a major cause of conflict. Even different speech patterns and voice can trigger responses that are unrelated to the reality of the situation. Being aware of misattribution is a big step in reducing conflict.

Western Styles of Conflict Resolution

The United States and other Western cultures have five basic strategies for resolving conflict.

1. *Win-lose (competition).* This is the strategy that seems most often used in Western culture. It alludes to a battle where one side wins and one side loses. While it has been used for centuries, relationships can be a casualty.

2. *Lose-win (acquiescence).* Here one side gives in, a "peace at any price" approach. While it can bring resolution to a conflict and on matters of little consequence may be most efficient, it can also devalue and create resentment in the one giving in.

3. *Lose-lose (avoidance).* With this approach neither party will initiate a discussion or action to resolve the conflict. The results are that relationships are wounded and conflicts go underground.

4. *Lose-lose (compromise).* Another way for both parties to lose is to compromise. The parties agree to "meet in the middle" but neither one wanted to be in the middle. However, receiving half of what you wanted seemed better than receiving none of it. Viewing this as a lose-lose seems to be a U.S. perspective. Many other cultures view this as a win-win.

5. *Win-win (collaboration).* In collaboration, both sides work to a solution that is not a compromise (meet in the middle approach) but one in which a totally new solution, fulfilling the needs of both parties, is mutually designed and accepted.

As you can see, each of these five styles takes the perspective of two sides in battle. Even in collaboration there is the underlying motivation of reaching the best resolution for each clearly defined side. Other cultures approach conflicts differently. Many times in multicultural situations, participants are caught off guard by the conflict and then seem unable to find a way to approach a solution. Learning these other strategies will give you additional resources to use and will help you recognize these approaches when you see them at work in your own multicultural environment.

Before we explore more effective crosscultural strategies, let's examine conflicts from a broad cultural perspective. David Augsburger, in *Conflict Mediation Across Cultures*, develops a framework for understanding different cultural understandings of conflict.[5]

Table 9.2. Different approaches to conflict resolution

Situationally defined conflicts (Options are open, pragmatic solution)	with	Culturally prescribed conflicts (Conflict is embedded in the culture's values and sense of right and wrong.)
Individual issues (Where the individuals involved have ownership of the problem)	with	Communal concerns (The group as a whole has ownership of the problem.)
Direct, dyadic approach (One on one processes)	with	Indirect, triangular approach (Third party processes)

As can be seen from table 9.2, these contrasts represent basic differences in cultural values. Reflecting on the different cultural lenses we have discussed, can you determine which cultures understand conflict in these ways? For example, individualistic cultures would fall into the categories on the left and collective cultures on the right.

Augsburger goes on to contrast the solutions to conflict as destructive (divisive) and creative (conjunctive). The destructive solutions result in alienation, competition, stalemates and denial. The creative solutions create bonding, connecting, resolving and re-structuring.[6] In a crosscultural situation, using strategies that are different than what you would ordinarily do may help you find a creative solution.

Crosscultural Strategies for Conflict Resolution

The following four strategies are adapted from Duane Elmer's book *Cross-Cultural Conflict: Building Relationships for Effective Ministry*, and will assist you in resolving conflicts in creative and mutually satisfying ways.[7]

1. Mediator, unwitting mediator. Most of us are familiar with the role of a mediator. What you may not know is that for some culture groups, using a mediator is considered the norm and the most appropriate means to deal with tension between two parties.

When a person from a culture that prefers mediators is living in the United States, it may be more difficult to enlist a mediator. The person who may have served in this role may not be living in the United States and the indirect messages that would normally solicit a mediator may not be understood by a U.S. American. In addition, the other party in the conflict may not be willing to work with a mediator.

Because of this, many times a mediator is recruited without being aware that he or she is being asked to serve in that role. Years ago a Nigerian pastor came to my office concerned about a problem between himself and another pastor. I listened very carefully, pleased that he would confide in me. When he was finished, I gave my best advice. He nodded in what I thought was agreement, thanked me and left. I felt so good that I had been of help. About a week later he returned to my office and told me about the same problem. Again I actively listened and suggested things that he could do. When he left I was curious about why he had come back, but reasoned that he must not have clearly understood my ideas.

Upon his third visit it became apparent that I was definitely missing something. Taking some of my own advice I sought the

counsel of a cultural coach, a respected Nigerian. He recognized immediately what was happening. The Nigerian pastor was trying to
engage me as a mediator, but I did not understand that. What appeared to be his unwillingness to solve the problem himself (that is,
taking my suggestions) was actually his earnest effort at bringing
about a solution (that is, obtaining a mediator).

2. *Storytelling, proverbs.* One of the best examples I know of
storytelling to resolve conflict is the story of King David and the
prophet Nathan. Rather than confront David directly, Nathan told a
story and then used David's own reaction to the story to open his
eyes to his behavior.

For many cultures this method of confrontation is most effective
because no one loses face. A person can make amends or rectify the
situation without ever having to orally acknowledge the offense. It
can also be used to create empathy or understanding of an emotional situation where it has been difficult to communicate feelings
successfully. Gary Smalley in *The Language of Love* recommends a
similar approach of using word pictures to communicate in a powerful but indirect way not for crosscultural relationships but for relationships within the family![8]

I have been amazed at how God can use this approach and variations on it to resolve issues that seemed otherwise irresolvable.
Once a very serious breech occurred in a crosscultural friendship
of mine. I knew something was terribly wrong, but could not figure
out what had happened, nor could I get my friend to tell me. I was
afraid that I would lose the relationship and never know why.

In desperation, I tried one last thing. I went to my friend's home
and asked if I could talk with her for a few minutes. She agreed and
I began to tell her a story about how I had been feeling. I had
thought ahead of things she had told me about her culture, what
she valued and experiences that had been meaningful for her. In my
story I related my feelings to circumstances she would relate to,
such as the loneliness of leaving all of her family to come to the
United States. I spoke of the confusion and deep pain of being

judged guilty of something without even being given a chance to explain, as those in her country who were forced to confess things they never did. As I was talking, she began to cry. Soon she was pouring out the hurt that had occurred and why she had blamed me.

Because we were able to talk about the situation, we grew closer rather than growing apart. My story did not accuse any one of anything. Rather, it allowed us to look at the emotions, create some common ground and work backwards to unwind what happened.

3. Inaction, silence, indefinite response. This approach is more subtle than some of the previous approaches. It may take more practice to become proficient at using and recognizing it. Indirect responses usually follow events or questions where the answer would be "no" or something negative. This prevents the use of "no" or direct confrontation, avoiding a loss of face.

For example, Ron asks Byung Kim to participate in a fund-raising event at work. Mr. Kim does not want to contribute, but rather than saying, "No thank you," he says, "I will try later." Ron does not understand that this is his polite way of refusing. When Ron continues to ask day after day, Mr. Kim becomes embarrassed and upset. He is not certain if Ron does not understand his answer or is just trying to humiliate him into doing what he does not want to do. If Ron persists to the point that he directly confronts Mr. Kim with, "Hey look, are you going to contribute or not?" as he might with someone from his own culture, the relationship will be damaged.

This type of scenario is common at all levels of communication and in all kinds of settings. The main thing to be sensitive to is the possibility that an indirect answer is actually a definite answer put in a softer form. This skill is acquired by listening to and observing other cultures.

Silence can also convey the same meaning. To a person familiar with other cultures, the silent message will be as clear as a verbal one. Take, for example, a meeting in which plans are being made for a special event. If the leaders of the meeting are from the dominant U.S. culture, they may assume that when ideas are presented and pursued those who disagree will speak up. Those from other cultures, however, such as many Asian cultures, will think that not verbalizing agreement or support will communicate that they are not in favor of the particular plan. It is important to tune in to the cues of silence when working crossculturally.

Inaction can also be a powerful communicator. For cultures where saying no directly is considered rude, inaction is often the way in which "no" is communicated. Persons from these cultures understand that you show respect by not directly refusing them. In other words, one does not need to say "no" when declining an invitation. Giving a "maybe," or "I'll try" will be sufficient, and the final answer will be delivered by whether you attend. While this may seem rude or confusing to Western thinking, it works well for the majority of the world.

4. *One down position and vulnerability.* This strategy is not new nor does it apply only to crosscultural relationships. All of us have probably been in situations where we have said, "Help me with a problem I am having" instead of, "You did not do what you said, and now we are having a problem." To put oneself in a vulnerable position by asking for help can be a tremendous asset in building and maintaining relationships, as can taking ownership of a problem so that the other party does not have to deal with the loss of face. A key factor to remember is that assigning blame and focusing on getting a person to admit error will most likely not be the best way to ultimately resolve the situation and maintain the relationship.

Being willing to try new approaches and strategies for solving conflicts will increase your ability to maintain relationships.

If you find yourself facing a conflict with someone of another culture and are not able to use any of the previous strategies successfully, you may want to try the following process, which has proven helpful in conflict situations.

1. Pray. This is always the place to start. Ask God specifically for wisdom to understand the other person's perspective, your misattributions and also the sensitivity to respond to God's leading in the resolution of the situation.

2. Identify behaviors, expectations and so on in the conflict. It is helpful to begin to sort out the areas of conflict. Is the conflict based on behavior—not adhering to a time schedule, speaking very directly and so on? Expectations—expecting to be rewarded for loyalty, expecting specific results, expecting a relationship to include particular aspects and so on? Values—desire for results, desire for relationship and so on? Once this is known the emotion associated with it can be seen from a new perspective.

3. Look for misattributions. With the areas of conflict identified, look for the misattributions. The behaviors, expectations and values quite probably convey a meaning to each party that is different from what the person thinks is being conveyed. Identifying the misattributions will help create greater understanding of the situation and may actually lead to a solution at that very point. Being willing to relinquish misattributions will be the more difficult task. The longer the history of the relationship and the greater the trust level, the easier this will be.

4. Clarify motives or salient cultural factors. Though important to clarify motives, this is often difficult to do. Asking "why" questions in situations can be too direct and sound accusatory. It is easier and usually more successful to ask the person(s) to describe what they have been wanting or how they would have wanted the situation to have been. Motives are usually discovered through this response, as well as salient cultural factors. Learning to listen in such a way so as to identify both motive and cultural factors impacting the situation will help the current situation and future relationships.

5. Diffuse emotion. Diffusing emotion has, hopefully, been hap-

pening through the entire process. God's leadership and the clari-
fication and understanding gained thus far should help the parties
feel calmer and more confident that a resolution will be found and
that the relationships will continue. It is important to remember
that resolution may well look different for each party involved. It
is not successfully achieved until everyone feels that it has happened.

In order for everyone to have a sense of resolution it may be necessary to give people a time to share what is in their hearts without
comment or rebuttal. Ground rules should be established for this
ahead of time and being flexible will be a key. Some cultures will
not be open to speaking from the heart and will want to placate the
authority figures involved, or they may want to use an intermediary
to speak for them. Allowing for these differences will help the process move along and will help build trust for the future. This is a
good time to check for any lingering misattributions.

6. *Find common ground.* In almost any conflict situation there
is common ground from which you can build a resolution. However,
it may not be obvious at first. Learn and practice discovering the
shared values, goals, relationships and so on, that you have with
others. Practicing this with those with whom you have no conflict is
a good place to start. Most people are amazed at how many things
they hold in common with others when they look for them rather
than for the differences. In the connecting exercises you will find
some ideas to assist you in developing this skill.

7. *Look for a long term solution, not just a quick fix.* Living in a
world of fast food, speed dialing and e-mail, you may also be used to
weighing the effectiveness of a solution against the speed at which
it can be implemented. You then decide what will give you the best
solution in the least amount of time. In crosscultural relationships,
when speed of implementing a solution takes a higher value than
saving the relationship, you have lost the war even if you manage to
win the battle.

It is also true that if you are accustomed to letting time solve conflicts—that is, doing nothing until enough time has passed to ease the pain or discomfort of the situation—then you may again be winning a battle but losing the war. In other words, it is important to keep in mind the relationship and the impact of this one event or conflict on its future.

8. Remember that mending the relationship is a solution. There may be times when keeping a relationship is more valuable than trying to dissect a situation or find who is responsible for a past experience. It is just as appropriate to work on not letting something happen again or finding better ways to communicate, clarifying roles or expectations and so on, than overanalyzing the past. Once opportunity is taken to share feelings, impressions and thoughts about an event, it is important to focus on the common ground and to move ahead with the relationship. Forgiveness can be given without being asked. Saying, "I am sorry this has happened" may help turn the corner so that you can move forward.

All healthy relationships experience conflicts, but by focusing on the relationship instead of just the problem, the relationship will not only survive but also grow stronger.

Connecting

1. Think about the conflict resolution strategies mentioned in this chapter. Name the two you use most often and why.

2. Select two new strategies that you are willing to try.

3. Read the following passages that Duane Elmer's book *Cross-Cultural Conflict* identifies and determine the conflict resolution strategy utilized.

John 8:1-11 _____

Matthew 27:11-14 _____

2 Samuel 12:1-9 _____

Matthew 21:23-27 _____

Mark 9:33-37 _____

4. Pick two relationships in which you are currently involved. (These do not have to be crosscultural relationships.) Make a list of the things you have in common. For one week, pick another person and think of the commonalties you share. List the re-occurring ones. How many of those same things would be true of a person of another culture?

For example, I have two friends, Jan and Lisa. The following are interests that we share.

Jan: home decorating, shopping, Bible study, crafts, travel

Lisa: volunteer at the SPCA (Society for the Prevention of Cruelty to Animals), movies, talking, shopping

Which of these could I also share with someone of a different culture? What other interests of mine would be shared by someone of another culture?

10

God's Heart for Crosscultural Relationships

"Real conversation is a treasure that seems all too rare these days.
When such opening of the heart occurs between people from radically different cultures,
it is a miracle of grace. This may be one of the highest aims
for which we were created. Each person, and each culture, has a unique secret.
Each is capable of knowing something of God which no one else knows.
In the meeting of strangers we have the opportunity
to share that treasure with each other."
BERNARD T. ADENEY

Maybe you harbor some doubts about the benefits of a multicultural world. You wonder if learning to relate to other cultures will ultimately produce a society where there is no understanding of right and wrong. Maybe, you think, it is our multicultural environment that is producing the "anything goes" mentality that seems so prevalent.

There are those who use multiculturalism to support a "no absolutes" philosophy. In fact, the only absolute to which some people hold passionately is that those with convictions of right and wrong should not be tolerated. This is absolutely not my position and not my purpose for writing about culture. God has given us absolute truths, which take precedence over all cultural beliefs.

God's truths do not vary from culture to culture. However, their expression and communication within a particular culture will be shaped and influenced by that culture. The Bible itself gives us examples of this truth. God sent specific persons—specialists, if you will—to reach certain culture groups. Paul, missionary to the Gentiles, adapted his presentation of the gospel depending on his listeners. Compare his sermon on Mars Hill (Acts 17:19-31) with his message to the crowds in Jerusalem (Acts 22:1-21). The truth did not change, but the method of expressing that eternal truth did change.

Biblical principles are universal, but when applied in a specific culture, they will reflect the values and priorities of that culture. The Bible teaches us not to steal (Exodus 20:15), yet how is stealing defined? In Matthew 12 Jesus and his disciples take grain as they walk through a field. The complaint of the Pharisees is not that they are stealing but that they are working on the sabbath. Their culture's priority was not dealing with picking someone else's crop, as many of ours would, but the violation of religious law.

In the Ten Commandments we read, "Honor your father and mother." This is a true principle for God's people, but the expression of that honor will be determined by one's culture.

The Bible teaches us to tell the truth (Ephesians 4:15, 2 Corinthians 6:7). We also believe Christ wants us to live in harmony, to be respectful and to maintain good relationships with others (Romans 12:16, 1 Peter 3:8-9). On some occasions our desire for honesty will take precedence over our desire for harmony and goodwill. At other times it is the other way around; it is culture that many times determines for us what is considered right in a specific situation. Because culture establishes what is appropriate, living in homogeneous culture groups reinforces our belief that our behavior is right. It also enhances our perception that behavior of those outside the group is wrong.

We use this principle to determine when we expect the truth and when we expect a culturally polite response. For example, if I ask,

"How are you?" and you say, "Fine," when in fact you are not, no one of U.S. culture will consider you a liar. Seldom do we expect a true answer when this question is asked in U.S. culture. It is seen as a polite question used as part of a greeting. Only among close friends or under special circumstances would we understand that a true answer was being requested. I have asked some well-respected Christian leaders if they have ever asked God to forgive them for lying to someone if they answered this question with "fine" when truthfully they were not fine. As yet I have not found one Christian who had actually considered doing this.

On the other hand, if I ask, "Are you a doctor?" and you tell me that you are when you are not, I will have a very different reaction to you not telling the truth. Cultural norms, values and their priority within your life make the distinction between the two.

Do we see Jesus making these same kinds of decisions? Look at the situation with the woman caught in adultery (John 8:3-11). In this situation there were different sets of priorities at work. Jesus never debates whether the woman was committing adultery or if the Pharisees were correct in saying that she should be stoned for such a sin. Jesus had a higher priority in mind: demonstrating God's forgiveness and grace. Sometimes the choices our culture would teach us to make are not the same ones God would have for us.

Culture impacts our application of God's truth, but does not change the absolute nature of God's truth.

God also knows and understands the impact our culture has on how we think and what we value and believe. Remember that God created us and knows us intimately. Our culture does not shock or surprise him. I believe God's purposes are fulfilled when the Christian community has the skills to relate to and build relationships with those of different cultures. And it is precisely these skills and genuine appreciation for all people that the world is desperately in need of finding.

How Did We End Up So Different?

The biblical account of the origin of various languages is the Tower of Babel incident recorded in Genesis 11. While chapter 10 indicates that other languages, families and nations existed, it seems likely that these languages were understandable between the peoples of the earth. It is not clear if these nations living over vast expanses of land were different culturally. A case could be made on both sides. But chapter 11 is clear. Because of humanity's desire to be like gods, those who had been of one language were made into many languages not mutually understood. Whether one interprets this account to be an actual event or the ancients' "story answer" to a puzzling reality, the meaning is exactly the same. It tells us that humanity's arrogance, pride and belief in self-sufficiency are the root of our primary difficulty with each other—our inability to effectively communicate and understand our fellow humans.

God created language and culture and can be honored and obeyed equally in any culture or language.

There are many interpretations as to why this division of language was necessary. Some speculate that it was a way for God to make sure that the world would not have to be destroyed again, as it was in the flood. Others believe that it was God's reaction to their sin of pride and self-sufficiency. For others, it may teach that human effort, no matter how great, amounts to nothing when done without God. Even for those who believe that it is only a story to explain what happened naturally through time and distance, the common truth remains. God created languages that would no longer be understood by all people. If there were not cultural differences before, they would develop now as the nations spread out and had less contact with each other. God created language and culture, but the creation of them does not give one culture more access to God and another less. We can experience God through any language or culture.

Since God Created Difference, What Does God Want Us to Do?

Knowing God created language and culture, it is interesting to observe that much of Scripture deals with issues related to the interactions of various cultures. Clearly God's desire is for his people to treat with respect and dignity those who are different linguistically and culturally, for example, Deuteronomy 10:19 states that God loves the alien (that is, stranger or foreigner). Leviticus 24:22 tells the Israelites that they are to have the same law for the alien as for the native-born. Numbers 15:5 says that God's chosen people and the alien are the same before God. Verse after verse gives instruction for the treatment of strangers/aliens and all the admonitions are to treat them fairly and honorably. (See appendix A for more Scripture references on aliens/strangers.)

As we look at our communities and those around us who are from another part of the world, speak another language or hold a distinct worldview as the "stranger," we also need to remember that as believers in Christ we too are strangers to an unbelieving world. In *From the Kingdom of Memory*, Elie Wiesel defines the stranger as "someone who suggests the unknown . . . the stranger represents what you are not, what you cannot be."[1] By acknowledging that strangers are not only "them" but also "us" we allow God to develop within our hearts and minds the perspective that allows us to grow in likeness to Him.

Jesus also deals with cultural differences and biases. One of the most famous parables—the good Samaritan of Luke 10:29-37—casts the person who was culturally different as the example to be followed. As Jesus and his disciples traveled through Galilee, Samaria and Judea, Jesus always treated people with respect, while recognizing their cultural perceptions and beliefs. How different would our country be if we too found role models in cultures and races different from our own and used those to shape our beliefs, rather than building our perceptions of others on negative encounters?

Later the apostle Paul writes, "there is no longer Jew or Greek" (Colossians 3:11). This teaching does not mean to nullify the im-

portance of these cultures but to emphasize the equality of all people in God's eyes.

Does Culture Impact One's Understanding of Scripture?

To understand and apply the Bible one must see it within the
framework of its culture. This is the basic principle of hermeneu-
tics, a fundamental course of theological training. One need not be
a theologian, however, to recognize how important understanding
the cultural context of Scripture is in grasping its true meaning.

The Bible clearly teaches that all persons have value in God's eyes.

Take any third grade Sunday school class studying the story of
Jesus healing the paralytic man (Mark 2:1-5). The teacher will
spend time explaining what life was like in the Middle East during
the time of Christ so the students will be able to put the story into a
context that makes sense. Without understanding that the homes of
that time had flat, thatched roofs the miracle of healing would be
overshadowed by the confusion about why these friends would cut
a hole in a neighbor's shingled roof and attic beams.

Understanding the cultural background and beliefs of the biblical
writers and their communities will help in interpreting any passage.
For example, the culture of Corinth is extremely significant in understanding Paul's letters to the church there. Understanding the
Gnostic influences and the leadership and moral issues of the culture help us apply the message to our own life circumstance. Many
theological controversies stem from how much Scripture and which
Scriptures should be interpreted through the culture of the time.
While scholars disagree about specific passages and the implications for interpretation, all Christians use the cultural/historical information to some degree as they discern, teach and apply
Scripture to their lives.

As one applies biblical principles to life, one's culture provides
the lenses through which the passages are understood. Reading

commentaries and Bible study materials written by Christians from a variety of cultures illuminates Scripture in new ways. Obviously this is not to say that the Holy Spirit cannot and does not illuminate Scripture to us, but rather that as the body of Christ we can help each other discern God's truth. Observing with our differing cultural perspectives is like looking out of a ship's portholes. What is seen from one porthole, while accurate, is not the entire view. We need to be in conversation with our fellow shipmates to get a fuller picture.

Robert McAfee Brown has written about the benefit of this type of engagement among Christians throughout the world. In his book *Unexpected News—Reading the Bible with Third World Eyes*, he gives example after example of how a biblical passage can be understood in vastly different ways depending on cultural and socioeconomic factors. He quotes Jürgen Moltmann in *The Church in the Power of the Spirit* where he says, "Reading the Bible with the eyes of the poor is a different thing from reading it with a full belly. If it is read in the light of the experience and hopes of the oppressed, the Bible's revolutionary themes—promise, resurrection and spirit—come alive."[2]

The readers' culture provides a lens through which Scripture is interpreted.

One example from Brown is the question "What does it mean to 'know God'?" The dominant U.S. culture answers this question with "those who have had some experience of God about which they are able to tell us." However, for José Miranda, a Mexican biblical scholar, to know God is to "do justice." This may sound strange to many U.S. Christians, or possibly even unbiblical based on the fact that so few Christians make "doing justice" a priority. Yet, an attempt to express a personal knowledge of God in words and not follow up with deeds, specifically the working toward justice, is incomprehensible to many from Latin American countries.[3] This concept of one's life showing one's faith is also clearly echoed in James 2:20.

Does God Desire Christians to Have Relationships with Christians of Other Cultures?

As Christians who are striving to be more and more like Christ, we know that there are values and behaviors in all cultures that are contrary to God's best for us, just as there are aspects of every culture that promote Christian values. Since the interpretation of Scripture and what it means to be a Christian is filtered through our cultural lenses, no one culture can be viewed as more Christian than another. In fact, we can all benefit by learning of and from each other's culture in our desire to grow in Christlikeness.

I met Samira several years ago through some mutual friends from the Middle East. She always amazed me with her hospitality, even when she was a student living on a very small income. There was never a time when she did not have something in her kitchen to offer people to eat and drink and she always did so with a willingness and joy that went far beyond just being polite. Hospitality is a natural and important element in Arab culture. I compare this to my own student days when money was also tight. Many times when guests came by, I had nothing but water to offer them to drink and no snacks whatsoever. The truth is, I never thought about trying to be prepared for visitors. My culture had not taught me the kind of hospitality that Samira's had taught her.

Which of the following cultural lenses do you think affect this difference between Samira and me?

☐ Context—high or low
☐ Authority—hierarchical or egalitarian
☐ Activity—doing or being
☐ Relationship—collective or individualistic
☐ Temporal—limited or abundant
☐ Worldview—premodern, modern, postmodern

What Does the Bible Teach?

The Bible is full of admonition to be generous and hospitable. Look at 2 Corinthians 9:6-8, Romans 12:13, 1 Timothy 6:18 and Hebrews

13:16. Whose culture, Samira's or mine, most encourages this biblical principle?

Another biblical principle often cited is found in Matthew 18:15-17. Here Jesus teaches believers how to handle grievances between themselves. Jesus teaches believers to go directly to the person who has offended them. Will this be more difficult for some cultures than others? For a low context culture this makes sense, even to those who know nothing of Scripture, but for a high context culture, this may be difficult to apply.

Christians can be challenged by their multicultural friends to become more Christlike.

God's Purpose for Allowing Multiculturalism in the United States
While many lament the changing demographics in the United States, it must be recognized as one of the most significant factors affecting world evangelization. People are immigrating, coming as students and business partners and so on, and are having the opportunity to hear the gospel for the first time. While many stay here permanently, others return to their homelands and share the life-changing relationship that they discovered. Those who stay form congregations compatible with their culture and language, or join existing congregations where they can build relationships not only with Christ but with their fellow believers. Many times in these and new ethnic congregations priority is given to mission efforts in their country of origin. More and more partnerships are formed between congregations in order to reach a particular people group, as a result of a relationship formed with someone from that country residing in the United States.

In September 1996 *Charisma* offered the following testimonials on the effect of work with internationals while in the United States.

> Ten years ago Robert Casaro, a Guatemalan studying at Mississippi State University, was so discouraged and lonely he dropped out of

school. He was at the airport ready to fly home when Christians from Maranatha Christian Church witnessed to him and led him to the Lord right in the airport.

Casaro stayed in school, graduated and went back to Guatemala to help plant a church there. Today, a decade later, the church has more than 1,000 members.

A campus minister befriended Francois Ayi, a Christian student from Togo, not knowing his uncle was king of a major tribe in Togo. The minister helped disciple and train Francois, who used his training to write a Christian bill of rights for his country. (Sadly, Togo now is ruled by a dictator, and the bill of rights is currently not in effect.)

Paul Wang and Winnie Li (not their real names) from Taiwan became Christians through the ministry of Churches Serving Internationals, headquartered in North Carolina. Now married, they will be moving to China where they will start underground churches in the communist nation and reach out to university students.[4]

The multicultural nature of the United States is a tool that can speed the spread of the gospel throughout the world.

But what about the multicultural nature of the United States with people who have been here for generations? Is God in this as well? Anyone who has lived in the United States for any length of time will have noticed the racial and cultural divisions that exist. As we discussed before the melting pot has not really happened. Instead it seems communities are becoming more and more divided. At election times politicians refer to the Hispanic, African American, Catholic and religious right vote, all perceived as having common cultural values and beliefs that unify them and set them apart from others.

But is this what is best for us? Is it what God had in mind? It is clear that among Christians this is not God's desire. Over and over we read of our need as believers to be unified. Colossians 3 tells us what our new life in Christ should be like. I once heard a speaker at a Church in the 21st Century conference observe that verses 5-10 deal with what we must leave behind when we accept Christ, and then verses 12-17 list new behaviors we need to adopt. The chapter turns on verse 11, the one that states that our new relationship as Christians means that we be conformed to our Creator and not let human differences divide us.[5]

What about those who are not Christians who are culturally, ethnically and racially different but live with us in our communities, our work place and our neighborhoods? Would the same mandates from God apply to these persons as to the stranger we spoke of earlier? I see no reason not to think so and every reason to think that it is exactly what God would want for his followers. What better way to show the power of God in our lives than to build relationship with those who are not like us? Is this not what Jesus did?

Connecting

1. Read the following poem. Do our cultural lenses blind us to aspects of who God is?

The Blind Men and the Elephant
It was six men of Indostan
To learning much inclined,
Who went to see the elephant
(Though all of them were blind),
That each by observation
Might satisfy his mind.

The First approached the
   elephant,
And, happening to fall
Against his broad and sturdy side,
At once began to bawl:
"God bless me! But the elephant
Is nothing but a wall!"

The Second, feeling of the tusk,
Cried, "Ho! What have we here
So very round and smooth and sharp?
To me 'tis mighty clear
This wonder of an elephant
Is very like a spear!"

The Third approached the animal,
And, happening to take
The squirming trunk within his
    hands,
Thus boldly up and spake:
"I see," quoth he, "the elephant
Is very like a snake!"

The Fourth, reached out his eager
    hand,
And felt about the knee:
"What most this wondrous beast is like
Is mighty plain," quoth he;
"Tis clear enough the elephant
Is very like a tree."

The Fifth, who chanced to touch
    the ear,
Said: "E'en the blindest man
Can tell what this resembles most;
Deny the fact who can,
This marvel of an elephant
Is very like a fan!"

The Sixth no sooner had begun
About the beast to grope,
Than, seizing on the swinging tail
That fell within his scope,
"I see," quoth he, "the elephant
Is very like a rope!"

And so these men of Indostan
Disputed loud and long,
Each in his own opinion
Exceeding stiff and strong,
Though each was partly in the right,
And all were in the wrong!

So, oft in theologic wars
The disputants, I ween,
Rail on in utter ignorance
Of what each other mean,
And prate about an elephant
Not one of them has seen!
—*John Godfrey Saxe*[6]

2. Do you think the following statement is true? Why or why not? "It takes all of us and all our cultural perspectives to begin to understand who God is." Does Revelation 7:9 shed any light on this issue?

3. Conduct a Bible study at your home and invite at least two persons (or two couples) from another culture to participate. Study one of the following passages and look for how cultural perspectives influence the interpretation and application of Scripture.

1 Kings 8:41-43

Colossians 3:1-17

Matthew 5:1-12

Romans 8:28-39

Romans 13:1-10

If that is not possible, select and study a book written by a Christian theologian from another culture.

4. Who are the "aliens" within your community? Look for all those persons who are powerless and without support.

5. Complete the following exercise.

Are You a Kingdom Thinker?

1. A family of a different culture or race moves in next door to you. You
   a. worry that property values will go down
   b. feel disappointed because you will not be able to have as good a relationship as you had with the previous neighbors

   c. get excited that you will have an opportunity to make new relation-
      ships that will stretch your world
2. When you see someone in clothing typical of another culture, you
   a. appreciate the beauty, gracefulness, creativity of the outfit
   b. wonder why they do not wear clothing more typical of your com-
      munity and why are they here if they do not want to fit in
   c. resent the fact that so many foreigners live in your city
3. You notice someone speaking with an accent. You are
   a. at the grocery store
   b. at church
   c. in the "wrong" part of town
4. A large, racially different family in a late model car is stopped by the
   side of the road, with obvious car trouble. You
   a. think that poor people should not have so many children
   b. stop to offer assistance
   c. want to stop, but fear an encounter with people of another race
5. In a local store you see three nativity sets. In one the figures have European features and coloring, in one they have Asian features and
   coloring and in the third they have African features and color. You
   a. recognize that each reflects people whom Christ came to save
   b. think that two of the nativity sets are inaccurate
   c. wonder why the nativity scene you identify with isn't good enough
      for everyone
Go back and think about your honest answers. If your answers were:

Question 1: a, or
Question 2: b, or
Question 4: c, or
Question 5: c,

you may be uncomfortable with difference and what you perceive to be a
threat to your sense of security. Do you feel less secure or more threatened
when you are around people of another culture or race? Do you think this
is something that pleases God? How do you justify those feelings? Are
those justifications based on prejudice or stereotypes? What truth would
God have you learn in relation to these beliefs?

   If your answers were:

Question 1: b, or
Question 2: c, or
Question 3: c, or
Question 4: a, or
Question 5: b,

you may be dealing with strong personal feelings about difference and a tendency to pass judgment without enough information.

Where do your strong feelings come from? What experiences have shaped how you think and feel about other cultures and races? Do those experiences give you adequate information to make judgments regarding a culture or race? Did Jesus in his ministry teach us anything about this kind of thinking? (For further study read Luke 10:29-37; Mark 12:41-44; Matthew 15:21-28; John 4:4-42.) Ask God if there are any changes he would like to see you make in this area and ask for his strength to do it.

If your answers were:

Question 1: c, or
Question 2: a, or
Question 3: b, or
Question 4: b, or
Question 5: a,

you are becoming a kingdom thinker. Watch for ways God will use you in the lives of others. Don't be surprised if he gives you opportunities to build relationships and share your faith with people from other cultures and backgrounds. Nurture the heart God has given you. Find ways to encourage others in their vision for God's world.

If you answered question 3 with *a* or *b*, know that you are in a community with opportunities to form a relationship with a person from another culture. Ask God to show you where to begin.

6. In *Multicultural Management: New Skills for Global Success,* the authors have listed a ranking of cultural values by businesspeople from six countries.[7] Look at their chart of cultural priorities. Rank these items for yourself in order of importance. Discuss with a small group of Christians how your priorities measure up to the priorities Jesus demonstrated in his life.

Table 10.1. Ranking of cultural values

Japanese	American	Malaysian	Russian	Swedish	French
Relationship	Equality	Family security	Family security	Freedom	Self-reliance
Group harmony	Freedom	Group harmony	Freedom	Relationship	Freedom
Family security	Openness	Cooperation	Self-reliance	Cooperation	Openness
Freedom	Self-reliance	Relationship	Openness	Family security	Relationship
Cooperation	Cooperation	Spirituality	Material possessions	Openness	Time
Group consensus	Family security	Freedom	Cooperation	Competition	Spirituality
Group achievement	Relationship	Openness	Spirituality	Self-reliance	Material possessions
Privacy	Privacy	Self-reliance	Equality	Privacy	Equality
Equality	Group harmony	Time	Time	Equality	Competition
Formality	Reputation	Reputation	Relationship	Reputation	Group consensus
Spirituality	Time	Group achievement	Reputation	Time	Risk-taking
Competition	Competition	Equality	Authority	Group achievement	Authority
Seniority	Group achievement	Authority	Formality	Material possessions	Group harmony
Material possessions	Spirituality	Material possessions	Group harmony	Spirituality	Cooperation
Self-reliance	Risk-taking	Competition	Group achievement	Risk-taking	Group harmony
Authority	Authority	Group consensus	Risk-taking	Group harmony	Privacy
Time	Material possessions	Seniority	Seniority	Authority	Family security
Openness	Formality	Privacy	Competition	Seniority	Seniority
Risk-taking	Group consensus	Formality	Privacy	Group consensus	Formality
Reputation	Seniority	Risk-taking	Group consensus	Formality	Reputation

11

Putting It All Together

"You don't have to move to Timbuktu to be a missionary anymore.
God is sending thousands of international[s] . . .
to the United States—and they each want an American friend."
ELISABETH FARRELL

Let's put it all together. How does what you have learned in this book affect what you will do in desiring, pursuing and developing relationships with people of other cultures? How will it affect how you share your faith or how you work together in ministry or in your community? We will explore those situations and others in this chapter.

Relationships

Perhaps you already have a relationship with a person or several people of a culture different from your own. Maybe this person is a neighbor or coworker, so the initial contacts are natural. But if you want some help to start expanding your circle of friends to include other cultures, this next section is for you.

Initiating a new relationship in our world of doing too much, too fast is always challenging. It is easiest when there are natural interests that draw people together. Many times we think that it will be hard to develop a friendship with someone whose culture and background are different than our own, but it is not as difficult as you might think.

Name your interests: your children, cooking, a hobby, sports, shopping, watching movies and dining out. You will find that there are persons from places and cultures different from your own who share these same interests. Begin looking for opportunities and ask God to guide you. Here are some ideas of places to start:

☐ Begin conversations at the next PTA meeting with the purpose of starting a friendship with a parent from another culture.

☐ Decide to cook an ethnic dish. Take your recipe to an import grocery store and ask for some advice from an employee or another shopper. You can take it from there. Find out about cooking classes or agree to teach each other. Plan to meet at a restaurant that serves that particular cuisine. Invite your new friend to your home to try a meal (maybe cooking your typical food or maybe trying theirs). The options are endless and the possibilities eternal.

☐ Volunteer for a fund-raiser for a cause primarily affecting another culture, for example, Sickle Cell Anemia, Human Rights in China, Native American policies and so on.

☐ Invite a coworker to lunch so that you can learn more about each other than your work.

☐ Have a neighborhood potluck, making sure every family is included.

Nurturing these relationships so that they grow deeper is far more challenging than making new acquaintances, but is more rewarding as well. This is where your understanding of the major aspects of culture is important. There are no easy lists of dos and don'ts because each culture is different and each person in that culture is also unique. As you have conversations and share experiences, you can observe your new friends' level of comfort with uncertainty, whether they view themselves more as part of a family/community or more as individuals and so on. Listen to the words they choose when referring to themselves. Read about their coun-

try of identity—you will learn a great deal and demonstrate interest
in them and acceptance of their culture. Always be yourself, but be
aware of the different messages that directness and indirectness
may send. (Directness may communicate aggression or disrespect;
indirectness may imply avoidance or lack of trustworthiness.)

Karen decided to initiate a friendship with the mother of one of
her son's friends from India. She was hesitant at first to be too
friendly, afraid that might make her seem suspicious. After some
casual conversations at school functions, she began to ask some
questions about India. Those conversations led to talk of Indian
food and what restaurants in town she thought had the best cuisine.
Sudha admitted that she was having a hard time adjusting to cooking American food, but her son liked it and wanted it especially for
his lunch. Karen suggested that they go together on a shopping trip,
both to the big chain grocery store and to the local import store
where Sudha purchased ingredients for her Indian recipes. It was
not long before the families were having dinner at each other's
homes and friendships developed between the husbands and children as well.

Doug noticed that a coworker from Brazil always seemed to eat
lunch alone at his desk. He knew that several people in the office
were not happy about Carlos being on their team and had made no
effort at befriending him. Doug worried that if he was too friendly to
Carlos, his other colleagues would resent him for it, which would
add to the tension already in the office and ultimately hurt his career.

One day when Doug went to the parking garage, he found that he
had a flat tire. Carlos was leaving at the same time and offered his
help, so together they changed the tire. While changing the tire
Doug asked Carlos a few questions about what he thought about living in the United States. It was obvious that Carlos and his wife had
not seen very much of the city and had not made many friends.

After Carlos's much needed help, Doug started looking for ways
to begin a relationship with Carlos and his family. They began with

shared meals in his home and trips to local sporting events. In time
the two of them were able to talk about their faith with each other
and grow spiritually through broadening their concepts of God.

Sharing Your Faith

The idea of sharing one's faith can be controversial in today's environment. For some interculturalists and cultural anthropologists,
respecting another culture means never wanting to introduce a
change, even at an individual level. Their reasons are understandable, especially in the area of religion, in light of how Christianity
has been introduced and conversions coerced during specific historical periods. They are right in recognizing the critical importance of religion in culture and wanting that respected. I too,
believe that respect is crucial, but respect does not mean that a person cannot choose to change beliefs. In reality, it is condescending
to withhold information because you do not want someone to
change; you are presuming to know what is best for the other person. Professor Darrell Whiteman of Asbury Seminary explains that
"Christianity does not destroy culture but transforms it."[1] How I
introduce my faith, the way in which I present the gospel, how I
demonstrate God's love and acceptance and so on, are the factors
that determine whether I have shown respect, not only for their
religious and cultural views but also for the person.

We have probably all heard of situations where well-meaning
missionaries have presented the gospel to groups of people and reported massive conversions. No one can be sure of the authenticity
of any single person's commitment, but by now you can recognize
the cultural factors that should be considered in this situation. For
instance, does this people group think of themselves in individual
or collective terms? What is the impact of being different from one's
family, especially in matters of one's religion? How do they respond
to being asked yes/no questions? Is saying no considered impolite?
What status do foreigners have? How do they show respect to foreigners?

It is important to understand these questions and their application when involved in mission work overseas. However, the same questions must be considered even when working within the United States. For all Christians the ability to effectively share Jesus Christ with others is a vital part of spiritual growth. (Effectively does not necessarily mean conversion, but rather communicating the gospel message in an understandable, appropriate way so that a person makes a decision based on the true meaning of the message rather than the form in which it was presented or the messenger.) It is especially true with our friends from other cultures because we may, in fact, present the first or only opportunity they will have to hear the gospel message. As we have already learned, the context of hearing the message may be as important as the message itself. This dialogue must be sincere and respectful of the other person's culture and beliefs.

Before you begin to open the doorway to faith conversations, ask yourself the following questions:

☐ Why am I doing this?

☐ Do I have something honest to say about my relationship with God, not just what I have heard others say or what I am "supposed" to say?

☐ Will I be able to listen to another's views on God without becoming defensive?

☐ Can I separate biblical principles from my culture?

☐ Can I allow this person's cultural expression of Christianity to be different from my culture's expression?

☐ Will it be all right if I cannot answer every question about salvation, Jesus, the Bible and so on?

☐ How will my relationship with this person be affected if he/she does not agree with me?

☐ Do we have the kind of relationship where we can disagree?

These questions are not meant to discourage you from sharing your faith, but rather to prepare you to be effective in your approach.

The following are some ideas for beginning faith discussions with friends of other cultures:

☐ Share your everyday relationship with God—answered prayers, Scriptures that comfort you or direct you.

☐ Ask about how their faith meets their spiritual needs.

☐ Offer to pray for them.

☐ Give them books or videos that tell a faith story.

☐ Discover their interests and find Christians with the same interests to include in your friendship.

☐ Look for Bible stories or biblical principles that teach a value which they respect.

☐ Don't be afraid to be honest about yourself and what it means to be a follower of Christ.

☐ Let God use you to demonstrate his love for them.

While it is important to share your faith, cultural considerations must be made.

Ministry

The word *ministry* is used a great deal in our society. *Webster's New World Dictionary* defines it in part as "the act of serving." Inherent in its definition are problems for the Christian wanting to be of assistance to those who are culturally different. Many times ministry involves an individual's or family's basic needs. The motivation is one of Christian love and service.

In order to minister effectively, however, it is imperative that those wishing to serve understand the cultural issues involved. In the next few questions we will explore some of those issues. But by no means will this be an exhaustive list. It is meant to prod your thinking so that in your particular setting and situation you will look for the salient issues involved.

☐ What are my beliefs about this culture? Do these come from stereotypes (outsider perspectives) or archetypes (insider perspectives)? Am I open to gaining a new understanding?

☐ How has the need been determined—through my culture's assessment or from the assessment of the culture being addressed?

In other words, is it a "felt need" from the people? Can the need be addressed through the group, either currently or by equipping someone to continue the ministry after an initial stage (the difference between giving fish and teaching to fish)?

☐ What are your expectations in providing this ministry? Do not be too quick to say "none," because we have them. They may be things like expecting those you serve to be grateful, consistent, wanting a relationship and so on.

☐ What expectations does this culture have for those who give help?

☐ What does the culture believe about and expect from those who receive help?

☐ How do members of this culture give and receive help among each other?

☐ Can a mutual relationship be established? "I would love to teach you English, but I would like to learn Thai. Would you be willing to teach me?"

☐ Are you willing to let the relationships transition into being more mutual and equal? With that in mind, what will need to be established from the very beginning?

☐ What training is needed for other volunteers in this ministry in order to have the greatest positive outcome?

Ministry can be the beginning of new healthy friendships, but only if the cultural issues are understood and addressed.

Starting a Church

There is much debate in Christian circles about starting churches based on the homogeneous unit principle which advocates starting churches by targeting people with the same culture, language, socioeconomic status, niche groups, subcultures and so on. I can remember having great debates with my fellow seminary students on whether this strategy violates the very essence of New Testament unity among believers. I stated boldly that God would have every church include anyone and everyone. Not only should they be open, but also be intentional in reaching out to their entire community, no matter what the race, creed or culture may be. To admit so blatantly our unwillingness to do so, under the guise of effective church starting, seemed dishonest at best.

My years of working with other cultures have broadened my understanding. I still believe that churches can be truly multicultural with shared leadership and the celebration of both our commonalties as well as our uniqueness. These congregations are examples of the Holy Spirit's work in our lives. God says that he desires that the barriers between us be broken down and that through our unity we will be known as his followers. The Bible is clear that in heaven we will be together, so it would seem to make sense to work together now. But are there other questions that need to be asked about this issue?

☐ Must all churches be multicultural to be biblically sound?

☐ Is the initial sharing of the gospel best done in an environment where one does not have to deal with cultural differences?

☐ Can a new Christian be discipled by someone from a different culture without mixing the teacher's culture with biblical principles?

☐ Will new Christians be given the opportunity to grow and exercise their gifts in a church where they remain a cultural minority?

☐ Can one be sure the message is understood if it is not given in a person's heart language?

☐ Would focusing on multicultural churches inhibit our support of the creation of new churches designed to reach a specific culture group?

By struggling to honestly answer these questions, I have decided that there are appropriate times to encourage the development of culture/language churches and times to encourage multicultural congregations. Both types of churches contribute to the body of Christ and our mission as his followers.

Let us turn our focus to the culture- or language-specific congregation. With God's leadership this can be the beginning of life-changing experiences for all involved, both within this particular congregation and with the sister churches with which they will relate. It is at this point of sister churches relating to each other, that mutual relationships, learning and growing, have their best chance of happening within the larger Christian community. Most important, though, it provides an opportunity for the people within the specific culture group to hear the gospel message and participate in meaningful discipleship. As Christ's body, the church—regardless of language or culture—is the way he has chosen to work among us.

All this potential, though, sometimes distracts us from the kind of planning and preparation that would help us see the greatest results. The following questions will provide some direction as you seek to know God's will in the area of church starting.

Why start a church? First and foremost the motivation and impetus for a new church must be with the Holy Spirit. Everything that is done from this point forward must be based on the knowledge that what we are doing is God's will, in God's timing. Experience has shown that unless a new congregation is based on this, it will struggle and make little difference in producing fruit in the kingdom of God, and can in fact make it more difficult later to begin the kind of congregation that is needed.

Pastors and leaders of ethnic churches need to be persons indigenous to and well respected by the community they will be serving. This may be hard to discern from an outside perspective (not part of that culture), so do not rely on your own insight. Seek input from others from that culture and observe their interactions together.

What do the demographics of the community tell us? Finding the demographic information needed can be rather simple or quite complex depending on your community and the target group you are working with. Census data is available in most public libraries and on the Internet, and periodic updates are available projecting population changes. Data is recorded for White, African American,

American Indian, Alaskan Native, Asian, Native Hawaiian, other Pacific Islander and multiracial.[2] In addition, there is a category for Hispanic or Latino and Race, with breakdowns of Mexican, Puerto Rican, Cuban, Other and White.

Your best information, however, will probably come from members of the group itself. It is important to know the size of the population and if there are any areas in town where there is a particular concentration of that people group. Understanding the history and religious background of the people group is also critical to a new church. With this data you will be able to plan the type and place of events and to notify the community of the new church.

For example, if you are working to begin a Chinese church it is essential to know pertinent information about the Chinese. Where are they from—China, Taiwan, Hong Kong, American-born and so on? What kinds of employment, education and family structure exist in the community? Strategic differences exist in reaching all the variations possible among the Chinese. The size of the community and the presence of other religious groups meeting in the area will also be important in determining strategy. Trying to build a church in a population group of under one hundred will be more difficult than in a group of ten thousand.

What does the culture tell us about approach, format and initial needs? Your understanding of culture will influence all decisions and will be crucial to the future of this new congregation. The six lenses we have discussed all impact strategy, methodology and leadership needs in a new congregation. In addition, the following questions need to be answered:

☐ What is their exposure and receptivity to the gospel?

☐ How strong are the cultural ties to another religion?

☐ Does this culture group have other Christian churches in the United States? What can be learned from their experiences?

☐ What kind of leadership would be culturally appropriate?

What assistance is necessary and how will it be given? This question, to a large degree, is answered by your ecclesiastical tradition and polity. Here are a few suggestions:

☐ It is important that both the new church and the supporting enti-
ties have realistic expectations. One of the first places relationships
can get off-track is in the area of expectations. Recall the concept of
losing face. Not meeting another's expectation is a common cause
of losing face. Sometimes even with a sure sense that God is in it
and with good planning and clear understandings, the growth of a
church may not go as planned. These discussions must be handled
with care. Do not imply blame, but work hard in your discussion to
be on the same team with the new church leadership.

☐ Provide counsel when it is requested, but be aware that a request
may not be a direct one.

☐ Always pray together, not just the perfunctory beginning and
ending prayers, but seek specific prayer requests and share yours
as well.

☐ Remember that the longer a new church receives outside financial assistance, the harder it will be for them to grow to be self-sup-
porting. While this may not be a concern to those supporting
bodies, ultimately being financially dependent is not healthy for the
congregation. I used to question if this was only true for some cultures, but after working with well over forty cultures within the U.S.
I have not found any that have benefited from prolonged financial
dependence.

☐ Understand what the support you are providing means or infers
to the new church. This may mean that you check with a cultural
coach from outside the church. For many cultures there are unspo-
ken expectations with the giving and receiving of assistance, especially financial assistance. The amount of help is a factor, but what
is determined to be large or small also has a cultural component.

For the U.S. culture, giving help carries with it the expectation
that the recipients will be grateful, show their gratitude verbally
and honor requests that are made to them by their supporters. Requests for additional funds after the agreement is made may not be
well received.

In the United States assistance is normally considered to carry little obligation on the part of the giver, except to keep the commitment to give. For other cultures, however, gifts or assistance can also obligate the giver. Understanding this can help make sense of some interactions that might otherwise seem illogical.

A large evangelical church in the southern part of the United States began a ministry with Ethiopian refugees twenty years ago. As time passed, many in the ministry came to know Christ and decided to start their own church so that they could worship and learn in their own language in a context comfortable for them. They went to the church that had been so gracious and kind in the past to ask if they would sponsor them in this beginning. After many discussions with the church leadership, they agreed to be the sponsors, which included paying the pastor's salary and miscellaneous church expenses for the first year.

Everything went well with the new church and their growth was steady. During the first year the pastor's wife lost her job and the church hired her to work in their childcare program. In addition, the pastor's car began to have major problems and it became necessary to replace it. When the sponsor church heard of this need, one family volunteered to give them a car that they were planning to sell.

When the leaders of the two churches met to discuss the needs for the next year, the Ethiopian church brought their projected budget for the next year. The sponsoring church thought that the growth in the congregation would mean that the Ethiopian congregation would begin to pay at least part of the pastor's salary themselves. Instead, they were requesting in the new budget an increase in financial assistance from the sponsor. The offerings collected by the church members were included but would be used for needed purchases such as a sound system, instruments, projects in Ethiopia and so on. Since the sponsoring church wanted to encourage growth and honor their initiative and planning, they agreed to the new amount for the following year, but asked that they not expect the same increase in the future.

By the end of the second year the congregation was averaging about 75 in attendance but the offerings remained small in proportion to the budget. At the year-end meeting with the sponsor the same scenario repeated itself. The Ethiopian pastor explained how hard it was to teach stewardship to his congregation because of their cultural history. The sponsor church leaders understood this and were so pleased that the church was doing well that they kept their financial support the same.

This scenario was repeated for five years. In addition to the direct assistance with budget needs, the sponsor continued to assist the pastor's family in the day-to-day situations that arose. While the church enjoyed the relationship with the Ethiopian church very much and wanted to continue having them meet in their facility, they decided it was time to reduce their support so that they could help another new church and so that the Ethiopian church could begin to be financially independent.

When this was discussed in the year-end meeting, the sponsor church leaders spoke directly, saying that they wanted to continue the relationship but that they would begin to reduce their support in the following year. They suggested that rather than the sponsor church paying the pastor's salary, that the Ethiopian congregation could begin doing so. By the sponsors giving financial support to the Ethiopian treasurer they could begin the process of becoming financially independent from the sponsor. The Ethiopian pastor was devastated and felt betrayed. His relationships with the sponsor church members and leaders became strained and he began to ascribe other motives to their behavior.

The sponsor church also felt confused and hurt. They had been faithful to this project and had gone beyond what they felt was their duty, and now they were angered by this response.

What actually happened here? From the beginning the two groups had very different understandings of what the relationships meant.

To the Ethiopian pastor, the sponsor church over time had reinforced his expectation that they would take care of him and his family. To state that they would no longer do so meant that they were breaking their commitment and changing the relationship. The pastor understood that he had lived up to what was expected of him as he continued to serve as the pastor. This sort of betrayal, he reasoned, must have been caused by something that he was not being told. He understood, from his cultural background, that there is virtue in disguising motivations, so he simply assumed that the sponsor church was not telling him their true motives.

To the sponsor church, the Ethiopian pastor had forgotten all that had been done for him and was now being ungrateful and unchristian in his attitude toward them.

Resolving a situation like this is difficult, and while the Holy Spirit is at work in each party, so are personalities and cultures. Both had tried to do what was expected to facilitate the development of the new congregation. At this point many churches would walk away from each other, feeling negative about what had otherwise been a great relationship. While this example referenced churches, it is equally true in personal relationships. Knowing that consistently meeting a people's personal needs can imply a relationship where they feel you are now obligated to continue meeting those needs, is a lesson less painfully learned from a book than from experience.

What could have made this experience turn out differently? It is hard to speculate with certainty, but let me make a few suggestions:

☐ Suppose that as needs arose in the pastor's family individual church members of the sponsor church helped them. This way the help would not always be from the same source.

☐ Suppose that these needs were addressed with a "teach you to fish" response rather than a "give you a fish" response. This may have been more time intensive at the beginning, but may have saved the relationship in the end.

☐ Suppose that the pastor and the congregation were involved in mutual sharing of resources (not all resources are financial) with their sponsoring church. Activities where the Ethiopian church was in the giving role would have helped to balance expectations.

☐ Suppose that the Ethiopian pastor had been exposed to church-starting situations similar to his own so that he would see what was considered normal in these relationships in the United States.

☐ Suppose that the Anglo pastor and other church leaders had received some cultural training about Ethiopian culture so that they would be aware of potential misunderstandings around the issue of assistance.

The list could go on, but the important point to remember is that there are options for solutions to most crosscultural difficulties if we are aware enough to know that the potential for a problem exists. When we find ourselves in a situation that seems to have no good resolution, it is usually because we did not even know we should be looking out for the possibility of a problem.

To effectively start churches in a crosscultural U.S. setting, it is essential that you identify the salient cultural factors and apply culturally appropriate methods and strategies.

Connecting

1. Select a project from the following list and begin making a difference in your life and in your world. Add to the list as God gives you ideas.

☐ Get involved with Voice of the Martyrs or other groups working with persecuted Christians around the world.

☐ Select and pray for an unreached people group. Unreached people groups are those identifiable ethnic/language/culture groups who have no sustainable Christian witness in their language. Organizations such as Adopt a People Clearinghouse assist churches and individuals with information and prayer requests for specific groups.

☐ Do a joint project with an ethnic church.

☐ Start an English as a Second Language class or International Friends ministry.

☐ Celebrate another culture's holiday.

☐ Begin a Bible study group with participants from a variety of cultures.

☐ Work on a Day of Reconciliation. Identify issues that divide your community and contact other groups that may want to work with you on identifying ways to resolve, forgive or reconcile.

☐ Host an international person for a holiday.

☐ Invite guest speakers to your church from different ethnic and cultural backgrounds.

☐ Visit art and cultural displays and museums and so on.

☐ Sponsor a games night featuring games and food from around the world.

☐ Develop a crosscultural friendship.

☐ Read a book about another culture.

☐ Read a book written by a person of another culture.

☐ Visit a store that caters to another culture.

2. The following are some ideas for crosscultural ministry. Think about the needs in your community. Work with others to find out what is already available and where you might become involved or begin a new ministry.

☐ Conversational English or English as a Second Language

☐ Driver's education

☐ Assistance with food, clothing and furniture

☐ Citizenship classes

☐ City orientations

☐ U.S. government/legal orientations

☐ Establishing country of origin clubs

☐ Establishment of country of origin choirs

☐ Developing a language (other than English) Bible study program

☐ Senior adult day time programs (a social outlet for people who live with adult children while their children are working and their grandchildren are at school)

☐ Job training

☐ Job placement training (résumé assistance, interviewing skills and so on)

☐ University tours for high school students planning to attend college

☐ United States culture classes

☐ Crime prevention workshops

☐ Health fairs

3. Think about one of your friends whose culture is different from yours. What cultural factors should you consider in presenting the gospel? See if you can find a Christian believer from that same culture who can talk to

you about what it means from their perspective to become a Christian. Ask God to show you ways to open discussions about faith.

4. If you are involved in crosscultural ministry, go back and answer the questions earlier in this chapter regarding your ministry. If there are changes that would improve those relationships, begin to take small steps to make that happen.

5. Think about ways in which you could train others in your church to better their relationships with those of different cultures within your community, using the concepts and information you learned from this book.

12

Just the
Beginning

*"Diversity can be a source of harmony, rather than a source of conflict.
Uniformity can destroy rather than advance civilization."*
DAVID AUGSBURGER

Throughout this book we have sought to explore the answers to the questions identified in the introduction.

☐ What are the keys to understanding culture and its impact on relationships?

☐ How does my culture affect my behavior, my beliefs and even my understanding of what it means to be a Christian?

☐ What is God's purpose in diversity of culture?

☐ How does God want his children to respond to a multicultural world?

☐ How can I become better able to establish and nurture friendships with persons of another culture?

Looking back at these questions now, let's see if we are ready to begin our journey across cultures.

What are the keys to understanding culture and its impact on relationships? There are six cultural lenses that give focus to our understanding of culture.

By understanding these six lenses and their impact on who we are and who others are, we will be better able to establish relationships with people from other cultures. Each person looks at the world through each of these lenses from a place that is both culturally prescribed and individually accepted. Once we recognize our own perspective we can begin to look at those around us and accept the perspective from which they see the world.

How does my culture affect my behavior, my beliefs and even my understanding of what it means to be a Christian? Culture gives meaning to all of life's experiences. It is culture that ascribes your value as you grow older or have children or receive more education. It is culture that shapes what it means to be a first-born or an extrovert. It is culture that teaches "how" you think and what you believe. Culture focuses life in such a way that we can view the world in a similar way as those around us, thus simplifying communication and interactions.

Figure 12.1. Six cultural lenses

Even in the arena of religion it is culture that shows us how we will process our experiences and derive meaning from them. As Christians, we may strive to have our values and behaviors shaped by biblical values and examples and an earnest desire to give glory to God, but even in those endeavors we are culture-bound.

How do we decide, for example, when the Bible speaks of trusting God instead of material possessions that it is all right for us as Christians to amass great fortunes for "rainy days" or retirement? Why do we believe God expects us to provide for ourselves before we help others or give to his church?

Why do we believe that God understands our lying to protect our "face" or our refusal to consider confronting someone directly with a conflict? How do we decide to spend hours in prayer yet not admit a mistake?

The answer is culture. Culture shapes how we prioritize scriptural teaching and its application to our lives.

As Christians we must look at Scripture, the culture of the times in which it was written, discern the principle being taught and apply it to our everyday situations. Yet we can only see Scripture through our human eyes, which see through the lenses of culture. Without the Holy Spirit intervening we would be unable to move beyond those cultural parameters. But the Holy Spirit does intervene in our hearts and minds to convict and challenge us to move beyond what culture accepts and find what God expects. With the Spirit's help we can refocus our lenses, change our cultural values, but this does not come easy or fast. Many Christians do not allow their cultural beliefs to be challenged.

Sharing your faith with a person of another faith and developing a friendship with a Christian of another culture are two ways to open yourself up to the Holy Spirit's work of challenging your cultural values and priorities.

What is God's purpose in diversity of culture? God created culture and the vast assortment of cultures present today are a reflection of his love of diversity. Duane Elmer says, "God can be properly revealed only through diversity."[1] That may be the best answer we have.

From my experience I know that there is a profound witness given when people from great diversity come together through the power and love of God. I have seen entire communities transformed when someone from a victimized or terrorized group has reached out to their cultural enemies, or when one from a warring nation repents publicly to those who have been attacked. His asking for forgiveness, not for his personal wrongdoings but for those of his countrymen, seems to release the power of God to break down barriers and begin a healing process. Without diversity we would not see God work in the human heart in this mighty and miraculous way.

How does God want his children to respond to a multicultural world? In the United States we have a tremendous opportunity to experience the richness of life by developing relationships with our neighbors who have come from cultures and countries unlike our own. The United States has the ability to provide a new home for millions of people who have come here for a multitude of reasons. While they may not have in mind finding a relationship with God through Jesus that might well be the greatest opportunity they receive in this country if we are willing to reach out beyond our cultural comfort zone. God wants us to embrace this opportunity as a gift from him.

We have a choice. We can respond with xenophobia—the fear of other cultures; ethnocentrism—believing one's own culture is superior; segregationist—wanting cultures to coexist separately; accepting—wanting others to become like us; or celebrating—learning from and enjoying the diversity of others. If we choose to celebrate the diversity God has created, the possibilities for his kingdom are great.

How can I become better able to establish and nurture friendships with persons of another culture? The answer to this question is the common thread woven throughout this book. Specific examples have surfaced in each chapter, but table 12.1 shows some general ideas grouped around the categories of attitudes, aptitudes, affinities and actions.

Table 12.1. Ways to develop crosscultural relationships

Attitudes	Aptitudes	Affinities	Actions
Be a learner.	Understand the cultural lenses.	Look for common interests.	Take initiative. Don't be too direct.
Show humility.	Know your own culture.	Find others who want to pursue crosscultural relationships.	Show interest. Trust God. Enjoy a meal together.
See God in the relationship.	Learn the cultural specifics of each culture you interact with.	Develop cooperative projects with other culture groups.	Share your own culture. Ask questions.
Focus on the relationship.	Develop observational skills.	Develop an emotional connection.	Be flexible. Pray.
Don't think your culture is best or try to prove it.	Learn appropriate ways to deal with crosscultural conflict.	Connect with the whole family.	Observe behaviors within the other person's cultural setting.

We live in an interesting place and time. As Christians we cannot ignore the opportunities all around us to be a part of what God is doing in our midst. The nations have literally come to our doorstep and we must be prepared to meet them, develop relationships and share the love of God. Not only is that our Great Commission, but it is what blesses our own lives as well. Go now with a prepared heart and mind and begin your own journey across cultures.

Connecting

1. What are the cultures that Jesus had contact with and what was his response? Why did he respond the way he did?

2. Mark where you are on the continuum for each cultural lens.

Context:	high ——————————————— low	
Activity:	being ——————————————— doing	
Relationship:	collective ——————————— individual	
Authority:	hierarchical ——————————— egalitarian	
Temporal:	abundant ——————————— limited	
Reality:	premodern ——————— modern ——— postmodern	

Do you reflect the archetype of your culture? Why or why not?

3. Think about one crosscultural relationship that you have. What will you do differently as a result of what you have experienced in this book?

4. What have you learned that helps you understand your behavior and values?

5. What is God asking you to do related to your multicultural community?

☐ Look for opportunities to develop crosscultural experiences.

☐ Read additional books on culture.

☐ Read about a specific culture with whom you have contact.

☐ Enlist a cultural coach.

☐ Develop a greater understanding of biblical principles related to diversity.

☐ Begin a crosscultural friendship.

☐ Nurture a crosscultural acquaintance into a friendship.

☐ Begin to train others to develop friendships crossculturally.

☐ Resolve a previous crosscultural experience.

Appendix A ◄ ....

Old Testament Scripture References: Stranger, Alien

Stranger

I am an alien and a stranger among you. Sell me some property for a burial site here so I can bury my dead. (Gen 23:4)

As soon as Joseph saw his brothers, he recognized them, but he pretended to be a stranger and spoke harshly to them. "Where do you come from?" he asked. "From the land of Canaan," they replied, "to buy food." (Gen 42:7)

My guests and my maidservants count me a stranger; they look upon me as an alien. (Job 19:15)

I was a father to the needy; I took up the case of the stranger. (Job 29:16)

But no stranger had to spend the night in the street, for my door was always open to the traveler. (Job 31:32)

Hear my prayer, O LORD, listen to my cry for help; be not deaf to my weeping. For I dwell with you as an alien, a stranger, as all my fathers were. (Ps 39:12)

I am a stranger to my brothers, an alien to my own mother's sons. (Ps 69:8)

I am a stranger on earth; do not hide your commands from me. (Ps 119:19)

Take the garment of one who puts up security for a stranger; hold it in pledge if he does it for a wayward woman. (Prov 20:16)

Take the garment of one who puts up security for a stranger; hold it in pledge if he does it for a wayward woman. (Prov 27:13)

God gives a man wealth, possessions and honor, so that he lacks nothing his heart desires, but God does not enable him to enjoy them, and a stranger enjoys them instead. This is meaningless, a grievous evil. (Eccles 6:2)

O Hope of Israel, its Savior in times of distress, why are you like a stranger in the land, like a traveler who stays only a night? (Jer 14:8)

Alien

The whole land of Canaan, where you are now an alien, I will give as an everlasting possession to you and your descendants after you; and I will be their God. (Gen 17:8)

"Get out of our way," they replied. And they said, "This fellow came here as an alien, and now he wants to play the judge! We'll treat you worse than them." They kept bringing pressure on Lot and moved forward to break down the door. (Gen 19:9)

Now swear to me here before God that you will not deal falsely with me or my children or my descendants. Show to me and the country where you are living as an alien the same kindness I have shown to you. (Gen 21:23)

I am an alien and a stranger among you. Sell me some property for a burial site here so I can bury my dead. (Gen 23:4)

May he give you and your descendants the blessing given to Abraham, so that you may take possession of the land where you now live as an alien, the land God gave to Abraham. (Gen 28:4)

Zipporah gave birth to a son, and Moses named him Gershom, saying, "I have become an alien in a foreign land." (Ex 2:22)

For seven days no yeast is to be found in your houses. And whoever eats anything with yeast in it must be cut off from the community of Israel, whether he is an alien or native-born. (Ex 12:19)

An alien living among you who wants to celebrate the Lord's Passover must have all the males in his household circumcised; then he may take part like one born in the land. No uncircumcised male may eat of it. (Ex 12:48)

The same law applies to the native-born and to the alien living among you. (Ex 12:49)

One son was named Gershom, for Moses said, "I have become an alien in a foreign land." (Ex 18:3)

But the seventh day is a Sabbath to the LORD your God. On it you shall not do any work, neither you, nor your son or daughter, nor your manservant or maidservant, nor your animals, nor the alien within your gates. (Ex 20:10)

Do not mistreat an alien or oppress him, for you were aliens in Egypt. (Ex 22:21)

Do not oppress an alien; you yourselves know how it feels to be aliens, because you were aliens in Egypt. (Ex 23:9)

Six days do your work, but on the seventh day do not work, so that your ox and your donkey may rest and the slave born in your household, and the alien as well, may be refreshed. (Ex 23:12)

This is to be a lasting ordinance for you: On the tenth day of the seventh month you must deny yourselves and not do any work—whether native-born or an alien living among you. (Lev 16:29)

Say to them: "Any Israelite or any alien living among them who offers a burnt offering or sacrifice . . ." (Lev 17:8)

Any Israelite or any alien living among them who eats any blood—I will set my face against that person who eats blood and will cut him off from his people. (Lev 17:10)

Therefore I say to the Israelites, "None of you may eat blood, nor may an alien living among you eat blood." (Lev 17:12)

Any Israelite or any alien living among you who hunts any animal or bird that may be eaten must drain out the blood and cover it with earth. (Lev 17:13)

Anyone, whether native-born or alien, who eats anything found dead or torn by wild animals must wash his clothes and bathe with water, and he will be ceremonially unclean till evening; then he will be clean. (Lev 17:15)

Do not go over your vineyard a second time or pick up the grapes that have fallen. Leave them for the poor and the alien. I am the LORD your God. (Lev 19:10)

When an alien lives with you in your land, do not mistreat him. The alien living with you must be treated as one of your native-born. Love him as yourself, for you were aliens in Egypt. I am the LORD your God. (Lev 19:33-34)

Say to the Israelites: "Any Israelite or any alien living in Israel who gives any of his children to Molech must be put to death. The people of the community are to stone him." (Lev 20:2)

Speak to Aaron and his sons and to all the Israelites and say to them: "If any of you—either an Israelite or an alien living in Israel—presents a gift for a burnt offering to the LORD, either to fulfill a vow or as a freewill offering, . . ." (Lev 22:18)

When you reap the harvest of your land, do not reap to the very edges of your field or gather the gleanings of your harvest. Leave them for the poor and the alien. I am the LORD your God. (Lev 23:22)

Anyone who blasphemes the name of the LORD must be put to death. The entire assembly must stone him. Whether an alien or native-born, when he blasphemes the Name, he must be put to death. (Lev 24:16)

You are to have the same law for the alien and the native-born. I am the LORD your God. (Lev 24:22)

If one of your countrymen becomes poor and is unable to support himself among you, help him as you would an alien or a temporary resident, so he can continue to live among you. (Lev 25:35)

If an alien or a temporary resident among you becomes rich and one of your countrymen becomes poor and sells himself to the alien living among you or to a member of the alien's clan, . . . (Lev 25:47)

An alien living among you who wants to celebrate the Lord's Passover must do so in accordance with its rules and regulations. You must have the same regulations for the alien and the native-born. (Num 9:14)

For the generations to come, whenever an alien or anyone else living among you presents an offering made by fire as an aroma pleasing to the LORD, he must do exactly as you do. (Num 15:14)

The community is to have the same rules for you and for the alien living among you; this is a lasting ordinance for the generations to come. You and the alien shall be the same before the LORD: (Num 15:15)

The same laws and regulations will apply both to you and to the alien living among you. (Num 15:16)

One and the same law applies to everyone who sins unintentionally, whether he is a native-born Israelite or an alien. (Num 15:29)

But anyone who sins defiantly, whether native-born or alien, blasphemes the LORD, and that person must be cut off from his people. (Num 15:30)

And I charged your judges at that time: Hear the disputes between your brothers and judge fairly, whether the case is between brother Israelites or between one of them and an alien. (Deut 1:16)

But the seventh day is a Sabbath to the LORD your God. On it you shall not do any work, neither you, nor your son or daughter, nor your manservant or maidservant, nor your ox, your donkey or any of your animals, nor the alien within your gates, so that your manservant and maidservant may rest, as you do. (Deut 5:14)

He defends the cause of the fatherless and the widow, and loves the alien, giving him food and clothing. (Deut 10:18)

Do not eat anything you find already dead. You may give it to an alien living in any of your towns, and he may eat it, or you may sell it to a foreigner. But you are a people holy to the LORD your God. Do not cook a young goat in its mother's milk. (Deut 14:21)

Do not abhor an Edomite, for he is your brother. Do not abhor an Egyptian, because you lived as an alien in his country. (Deut 23:7)

Do not take advantage of a hired man who is poor and needy, whether he is a brother Israelite or an alien living in one of your towns. (Deut 24:14)

Do not deprive the alien or the fatherless of justice, or take the cloak of the widow as a pledge. (Deut 24:17)

When you are harvesting in your field and you overlook a sheaf, do not go back to get it. Leave it for the alien, the fatherless and the widow, so that the LORD your God may bless you in all the work of your hands. (Deut 24:19)

When you beat the olives from your trees, do not go over the branches a second time. Leave what remains for the alien, the fatherless and the widow. (Deut 24:20)

When you harvest the grapes in your vineyard, do not go over the vines again. Leave what remains for the alien, the fatherless and the widow. (Deut 24:21)

When you have finished setting aside a tenth of all your produce in the third year, the year of the tithe, you shall give it to the Levite, the alien, the fatherless and the widow, so that they may eat in your towns and be satisfied. (Deut 26:12)

Then say to the LORD your God: "I have removed from my house the sacred portion and have given it to the Levite, the alien, the fatherless and the widow, according to all you commanded. I have not turned aside from your commands nor have I forgotten any of them." (Deut 26:13)

"Cursed is the man who withholds justice from the alien, the fatherless or the widow." Then all the people shall say, "Amen!" (Deut 27:19)

The alien who lives among you will rise above you higher and higher, but you will sink lower and lower. (Deut 28:43)

Any of the Israelites or any alien living among them who killed someone accidentally could flee to these designated cities and not be killed by the avenger of blood prior to standing trial before the assembly. (Josh 20:9)

His master replied, "No. We won't go into an alien city, whose people are not Israelites. We will go on to Gibeah." (Judg 19:12)

David said to the young man who brought him the report, "Where are you from?" "I am the son of an alien, an Amalekite," he answered. (2 Sam 1:13)

To whom alone the land was given when no alien passed among them . . . (Job 15:19)

My guests and my maidservants count me a stranger; they look upon me as an alien. (Job 19:15)

Hear my prayer, O LORD, listen to my cry for help; be not deaf to my weeping. For I dwell with you as an alien, a stranger, as all my fathers were. (Ps 39:12)

I am a stranger to my brothers, an alien to my own mother's sons. (Ps 69:8)

You shall have no foreign god among you; you shall not bow down to an alien god. (Ps 81:9)

They slay the widow and the alien; they murder the fatherless. (Ps 94:6)

Then Israel entered Egypt; Jacob lived as an alien in the land of Ham. (Ps 105:23)

The LORD watches over the alien and sustains the fatherless and the widow, but he frustrates the ways of the wicked. (Ps 146:9)

The LORD will rise up as he did at Mount Perazim, he will rouse himself as in the Valley of Gibeon—to do his work, his strange work, and perform his task, his alien task. (Is 28:21)

If you do not oppress the alien, the fatherless or the widow and do not shed innocent blood in this place, and if you do not follow other gods to your own harm, . . . (Jer 7:6)

This is what the LORD says: Do what is just and right. Rescue from the hand of his oppressor the one who has been robbed. Do no wrong or violence to the alien, the fatherless or the widow, and do not shed innocent blood in this place. (Jer 22:3)

When any Israelite or any alien living in Israel separates himself from me and sets up idols in his heart and puts a wicked stumbling block before his face and then goes to a prophet to inquire of me, I the LORD will answer him myself. (Ezek 14:7)

In you they have treated father and mother with contempt; in you they have oppressed the alien and mistreated the fatherless and the widow. (Ezek 22:7)

The people of the land practice extortion and commit robbery; they oppress the poor and needy and mistreat the alien, denying them justice. (Ezek 22:29)

"In whatever tribe the alien settles, there you are to give him his inheritance," declares the Sovereign LORD. (Ezek 47:23)

I wrote for them the many things of my law, but they regarded them as something alien. (Hosea 8:12)

Do not oppress the widow or the fatherless, the alien or the poor. In your hearts do not think evil of each other. (Zech 7:10)

Appendix B ◄ ·

Culture/Feature Chart

Power Distance—PD   Uncertainty Avoidance—UA
Collective—C   Individualistic—I
Doing—D   Being—B

Features of different cultures in the world

India	Large PD	Low UA	C	D
Indonesia	Small PD	Low UA	C	B
South Africa	Large PD	Low UA	I	D
Mexico	Large PD	High UA	C	D
Korea	Large PD	High UA	C	B
Italy	Small PD	High UA	I	D
France	Large PD	High UA	I	B
Costa Rica	Small PD	High UA	C	B
United States	Small PD	Low UA	I	D
Finland	Small PD	Low UA	I	B
New Zealand	Small PD	Low UA	I	D
Sweden	Small PD	Low UA	I	B

Compiled from Geert Hofstede's work in *Culture's Consequences: International Differences in Work-Related Values*. Beverly Hills, Calif.: Sage, 1980.

Appendix C ◄ ....

Preparing to Share
Your Faith Across Cultures

1. Write how you might share your Christian faith with someone.

2. Look at the words you used and needs you addressed. Do you see any of your cultural features reflected? What aspects of your culture did you reflect? Discuss this with another Christian.

3. Select a culture group by selecting a combination of cultural features.

You may put together any combination that you would like. Examples of countries with the different profiles are in appendix B. You should circle one item on each line.

Large Power Distance   Small Power Distance
High Uncertainty Avoidance   Low Uncertainty Avoidance
Individual   Collective
Doing   Being

(You may also want to think in terms of high and low context.)

4. Thinking about this culture group, how would your presentation communicate? How would you change it to communicate better?

Appendix D ◄ ....

Preparing to Minister
Within a Diverse Community

All of us have a culture, which impacts our view of the world and our relationships with others. Our culture tells us what is kind and what is offensive, what is appropriate and what is not, even what is reality.

As we work with persons from a culture different than ours—and that may be happening even if there are no visible signs of a difference—we can develop better relationships if we recognize the impact of culture. Many times people believe that culture is determined by race or geography, but in reality culture is a system of meanings and values that shape our behavior and beliefs.[1] It is passed down from generation to generation and reinforced by the larger community. All culture is dynamic, but some cultures make rapid changes and others change very slowly. A population group could look all the same on the outside but their cultures could be very different.

The following questions will help you identify some important information about culture. The answers and explanations will follow.

❊   ❊   ❊

1. Everyone has a culture.

                              True   False

2. There is a basic human culture that we all have.

                              True   False

3. Culture consists of language, clothing, forms of greetings and foods.

                              True   False

4. All cultures have areas of sensitivity and ways they can be offended, as well as offend.

                              True   False

5. Everyone from the same country has the same culture.

                              True   False

6. The best culture in the world today is the dominant U.S. culture.

                              True   False

7. Diversity within an organization/church decreases its productivity because unity can not be achieved.

                              True   False

8. As Christians, we leave our cultural values as we apply God's values to our lives.

                              True   False

9. Christians from other cultures may have greater insight into some biblical passages due to their cultural perspective and history.

                              True   False

10. Most people find it difficult to identify their own culture because cultural values are so deeply embedded they seem to be innate human beliefs.

                              True   False

❊   ❊   ❊

Answers

1. True. There are no culture-free persons. Each of us has learned a system of meanings and values that shape our behavior and beliefs. This is our culture. People can vary greatly within a culture depending on their individual education, temperament/personality type, spiritual development and so on. One's culture provides the bedrock for all other influences on us, including faith.

2. False. We all share human needs, emotions, characteristics. What evokes our emotions depends, in part, on our culture and what may seem normal in one culture may be considered deviant in another culture. Real problems can arise when we attribute motive or meaning to a behavior based on our culture's perspective. It is a good idea to check with someone from that culture group to determine what the behavior would mean to them. For example, a person who speaks softly and does not make eye contact may be indicating shyness or respect. It depends on his/her culture.

3. True, but incomplete. Culture is more than these visible elements. It also includes one's beliefs, values, motivations and worldview. The visible part of culture is objective culture, the invisible is subjective culture and it is the motivation for the visible aspects. It is much easier to change objective culture than it is to change subjective. Many times people believe they (or someone else) have assimilated into the dominant culture because objective culture has changed. Most people do not ever make major changes in their subjective culture.

4. True. It may be easier to see the sensitivity of others than to see our own. It is also true that history, minority/majority status, perception of power impact a culture's sensitivity. There are always unique individual differences.

5. False. Every culture has subcultures or microcultures. Think for a minute about the cultures within the U.S.-born population. Even organizations have cultures. Remember culture is a system of meanings and values that shape one's behavior. However, general statements can be made about culture groups. These are called

archetypes. They differ from stereotypes in that they are

☐ from an insider perspective (someone of that culture)

☐ nonrestrictive (not prescribing boundaries or limitations)

☐ nonaccusative (not accessing a fault or deficiency)

Also, remember just as you know from interaction with those from your own culture, there are great variations within cultures. Cultural values are expressed in various ways and to various degrees.

The term "U.S. dominant culture" refers to Anglo, middle-class. A dominant culture is not necessarily the majority, but rather the culture that is reflected in the societal structures.

6. False. Best to whom? There are positive aspects of each culture and some cultures are better suited for different environments than the dominant U.S. culture. As with most things, each positive has a corresponding negative. For example, the U.S. culture emphasizes each person reaching his/her potential, yet that same value may breed selfishness and self-centeredness. Some cultures promote loyalty as a high value, yet that loyalty may mean that truth is ignored.

7. False. Unity may be more difficult to achieve, but in the process the varied perspectives will help locate potential problems and blind spots not otherwise seen.

8. False. Our culture impacts how we understand ourselves to be Christians and how we understand Scripture. All of us are prone to interpret the Bible through our cultural lenses and to mingle our own cultural preferences with biblical teaching. Christians from various cultures serve one another and the cause of Christ by joining in prayer and discussion on these matters. We do not leave our culture, but rather let God's word and Spirit change us and our cultural beliefs.

9. True. Who better than an Arab Muslim who has become a Christian to share the meaning of "whoever would follow me must leave his father and mother"? Who better than an African refugee to know how the "Son of Man had no home"? There are many in-

sights into Scripture that are hidden from us. Either our culture creates blinders through which we cannot readily see the true impact of the passage, or we are so unfamiliar with the cultural value reflected in the passage, that we miss some of the message that God has for us.

10. True. By definition, culture consists of those values and beliefs learned from birth and are seldom, if ever, questioned.

Appendix E

How Does Culture Influence Your Values?

Select the response that most reflects your feelings:

1. Which of these situations would be the most confusing?

   a. Being asked to attend a meeting but not knowing why.

   b. Being told you were a friend but never invited to that person's home.

   c. Being asked to be in charge of a function but not having the authority to make decisions pertaining to it.

   d. Being told your pastor also drives a truck for additional income.

2. Which of these actions would seem the rudest?

   a. Someone asking you how much you paid for an item.

   b. Someone handing you a gift using only one hand.

   c. Someone not showing up for an appointment with you and not calling to explain why.

      d. Someone stopping you in a store to ask your opinion of a
      dress they were thinking of buying.
   3. Who should have the most authority in society?
      a. The elected officials
      b. The eldest or ascribed leaders
      c. The most educated/knowledgeable
      d. The ones with the most money/power
   4. Which of these would be the correct response?
      a. Yes
      b. What the one asking wanted you to say
      c. Your opinion
      d. What your parents thought
   5. Who has the most control of what happens to you?
      a. The government
      b. Your family
      c. Yourself
      d. Nature/fate

These questions deal with issues including:

   1. Uncertainty, lack of power, friendship and status
   2. Manners and signs of respect
   3. Status, both achieved and ascribed
   4. "Saving face" and honor
   5. Worldview

You may want to use these questions with some of the people
you know who are from a different culture. You will learn a great
deal about the values you have in common and those that you do
not, and it can help in building a greater understanding of one
other.

Cultures differ greatly in all of these areas. It is important that as
work is done interculturally, sensitivity is developed to the differences so that avoidable barriers will not impede the relationship,
which is key to effective ministry. The following acrostic shares
some good ideas on what can be done to nurture a crosscultural relationship.

R	E	L	A	T	I	O	N	S	H	I	P
E	M	E	C	R	N	P	U	E	E	N	R
A	P	A	C	U	T	E	R	R	A	C	A
C	A	R	E	S	E	N	T	V	R	L	Y
H	T	N	P	T	R		U	E		U	
	H		T		C	U	R			D	
O	I				E	P	E			E	
U	Z				D						
T	E				E						

Appendix F

Building
Intercultural
Relationships

Complete each phrase by choosing one of the following options that would best reflect your action in the given situation.

1. When your new neighbor is from the Middle East, do you

   a. Go over and ask many questions about her background, beliefs, religion, and so on, to show her how interested you are in her?

   b. Wait to see if she comes to see you?

   c. Take a "sweet" and offer to answer her questions or help with knowing her way around the area?

2. You meet a woman who looks Asian in the doctor's waiting room, do you

   a. Ask her where she is from?

   b. Stare at her until she notices you and then say how wonderful you think it is that Orientals are so petite?

   c. Begin a normal conversation with her as you would anyone else?

3. When you mentor a student who lives in a less affluent area than you, do you

   a. Assume he/she wants to be like you—have your values and lifestyle?

b. Value his/her life experiences and affirm their value in God's eyes?

c. Verbalize your surprise/distress over the student's family or living situation so the student will see your compassion?

4. When you are teaching English to a person born outside the United States, do you

a. Focus on building a meaningful relationship that is mutual?

b. Focus on maximizing the English skill acquired?

c. Focus on converting her/him to Christianity?

5. When the mother you are teaching in the job-training program asks you for advice on dealing with her child's school problem, do you

a. Explain how important education is to living the American Dream?

b. Tell her the problems you had with your child in school and how the answer had been home schooling?

c. Listen to what she thinks the real problem is and offer to assist/support her in the resolution of it?

Answers

1. c   2. c   3. b   4. a   5. c

Explanations

1. Even though answer *a* may come naturally to us, it will not show interest in her, but rather be seen as too invasive and may even be a barrier to a later relationship. Answer *b* may result in no relationship at all and would probably communicate rejection. Answer *c* shows hospitality and a willingness to be a friend, without invading areas of life where acquaintances are not welcome.

2. Many people begin conversations with others who look like they are from a different part of the world by asking them where they are from. While many times there is no problem with this, there are those times when people are offended. This could be because the people believe that you are asking because you disapprove of them. Also, people could be afraid, especially if their immigration status is not in order or if they are from a country where persecution or government intervention is common. And sometimes the offense comes because people think the question reveals that you have stereotyped them. Answer *b* reflects what sometimes happens without our knowing it. We are genuinely interested in talking to a person, but get caught staring at him/her and then make an awkward attempt at conversation. *C* is the best option to begin a conversation that could lead to a friendship.

3. We can never assume that our way of life is what others would like to have, no matter how successful or happy we might be. Many see the dominant U.S. culture as oppressive, lacking real emotion, materialistic, frantic and so on. Others may see conforming to the establishment as selling out and denying their heritage. To assume that we have what others want puts us in a superior position and comes across as arrogant, which ultimately will negatively impact our relationship. Answer *c*, while communicating sympathy, again will put you in a position of superiority and may appear judgmental.

Answer *b* is the best option for building a relationship and sharing God's love.

4. While increasing English skills is the course objective and is important, we can use teaching methods that accomplish that but lose the relationship and ultimately the student. We must be careful when designing our teaching activities to use those that are positive and culturally appropriate. If we emphasize winning someone to Christ, we risk misunderstandings and alienation. By focusing on a mutual relationship it is possible to accomplish all three (friendship, English skill and coming to know Christ).

5. While both *a* and *b* may have some usefulness in a conversation, it is *c* that will be most helpful. There is a wealth of healing in truly being heard and having your opinions valued. With the right encouragement, she will know a great deal about how to solve the situation herself and it will be much more effective coming from her.

Appendix G ◂ . . . .

Checklist for Intercultural Church Relationships

Goal	Method
Understand your cultural beliefs and values.	1. Answer questionnaire (see chapter two). 2. Look at the values expressed in idioms. 3. Discuss "Observations from Foreign Visitors."*
Understand the other culture's beliefs and values.	1. Read a book about the other culture written by someone of the culture. 2. Have someone from the culture come and speak on the culture. 3. Attend a cultural awareness conference or training session.
Develop consensus on what you expect from each other.	1. Pray about your expectations. 2. Write/outline your expectations. 3. Discuss the expectations together. 4. Determine if these can be met by the other. 5. Agree to meet these for a set time period and then evaluate.

* From Robert C. Kohls and John M. Knight "Developing Intercultural Awareness—A Cross-Cultural Training Handbook" Yarmouth, Me: Intercultural Press, 1994.

Develop consensus on what you will work together to do.	1. Discuss what you both want to accomplish. 2. Recognize and value the cultural values represented in each culture. 3. Agree to assist each other in the accomplishment of goals. 4. Plan what actions need to be taken.
Fellowship together often.	1. Pray together. 2. Share a meal together (pot luck, in homes, in restaurants). 3. Work on joint projects.
Identify a course of action if a concern arises among one or both groups or individuals.	1. Explain how each group deals with conflict and why. 2. Agree on the steps each will take if a problem arises. 3. Notify those involved what the process will be.
Alternate or share leadership roles.	1. Create situations for leadership to be shared or alternated. 2. Show Christlike humility as a leader.

Notes

Introduction

[1]Larke Nahme Huang and Sara Nieves-Grafals, "Cross-Cultural Counseling" (lecture given at the National Multicultural Institute, Washington, D.C., November 3-4, 1994).

[2]Geert Hofested, *Culture's Consequences: International Differences in Work-Related Values* (Beverly Hills, Calif.: Sage, 1980), p. 25.

[3]Harry C. Triandis, Pierre K. Dadsen and Alastair Heron, "Cross-Cultural Tests of Piaget's Theory," in *The Handbook of Cross-Cultural Psychology,* ed. William Wilson Lambert (Boston: Allyn & Bacon, 1980), 4:298.

[4]Ibid.

Chapter 1: What Is Our Cultural Landscape?

[1]Interdev, U.S. Census Bureau, American Demographics, *U.S.A. Today,* Operation World, World Advance, *Seattle Post Intelligence,* Iranian Christians International. Quoted in *Charisma,* October 1997, p. 57.

[2]Larke Nahme Huang and Sara Nieves-Grafals, "Cross-Cultural Counseling" (lecture given at the National Multicultural Institute, Washington, D.C., November 3-4, 1994).

[3]An immigrant is a person from another country who desires to make a home in the United States. A person can qualify to be an immigrant in many ways and may apply in their country or while in the United States. A refugee is also an immigrant, usually settled in the United States by a refugee resettlement agency. The U.S. government limits the number of refugees and other immigrants processed into the United States each year. International students receive an F1 visa that allows them to live in the United States while attending an approved college or university. An international businessperson receives a B1 visa that allows them to reside in the United States for a specific amount of time to conduct business.

[4]Huang and Nieves-Grafals, "Cross-Cultural Counseling" lecture.

[5]Graham E. Fuller, *Secrets of Learning a Foreign Language* (Carlsbad, Calif.: Penton Overseas, Inc., 1992), audio cassette.

[6]Third Culture Kids, ed. Ruth Hill Useem (November 2001), TCK World <www .tckworld.com/useem/tckbibbook.html>.

[7]1.5 generation refers to children who moved to a new country when they were young—thus educated in the United States, for example. However, they are not truly a second generation since they were not born in the United States. American-born is a term often used to refer to second generation, as in American-born Chinese.

[8]Gamma Vision, Inc., "Culturally-Based Patterns of Difference" (Kochman Communication Consultants, Ltd., San Francisco, Calif., 1989, photocopied handout).

[9]Ibid.

[10]Huang and Nieves-Grafals, "Cross-Cultural Counseling" lecture.

Chapter 2: Do You Understand Your Own Culture?

[1]Darrell Whiteman, "Culture, Values, and Worldviews: Anthropology for Mission Practice" (lecture given at the Overseas Ministries Study Center in New Haven, Conn., 1999).

[2]Nancy Barger, Tom Flautt, and Helen Pelikan, facilitators, "Interplay of Culture and Type." (discussion at the conference for Successfully Applying the Myers-Briggs Type Indicator in Multicultural Setting; presented by the Pelikan Associates in Denver Colo., April 27-29, 1992).

[3]Isabel Briggs Myers, Mary H. McCaulley, Naomi L. Quenk and Allen L. Hammer, *MBTI Manual A Guide to the Development and Use of the Myers-Briggs Type Indicator,* Third Edition. (Palo Alto, Calif.: Consulting Psychologists, 1998), p. 380.

[4]Paul Pedersen and Allen Ivey, *Culture Centered Counseling and Interviewing Skills* (Westport, Conn.: Praeger, 1993), pp. 76-81, permission granted.

[5]Robert Singh, *The Farrakhan Phenomenon–Race, Reaction, and the Paranoid Style in American Politics* (Washington, D.C.: Georgetown University Press, 1997), pp. 101-2.

Chapter 3: Where Are We?

[1]Edward T. Hall, *Beyond Culture* (Garden City, N.Y.: Anchor/Doubleday, 1976), p. 75.

[2]Jaime S. Wurzel and Nancy K. Fischman, *A Different Place: The Intercultural Classroom* (Newtonville, Mass.: Intercultural Resource Corporation, 1994), pp. 38-43.

[3]Ibid.

[4]This illustration is based on interviews with many people who work in multicultural settings. You will find similar dialogues in a book by Craig Storti, *Cross-Cultural Dialogues* (Yarmouth, Maine: Intercultural Press, 1994).

[5]Wurzel and Fischman, *A Different Place*, pp. 38-43.

Chapter 4: What Drives Us?

[1]Jaime S. Wurzel and Nancy K. Fischman, *The Intercultural Classroom* (Newton-

ville, Mass.: Intercultural Resource Corporation, 1994), p. 23.

[2]Joanne Zitek and Cynthia Livingston, "Coaching and Giving Feedback in Multicultural Organizations" (lecture given at SIETAR International Congress in Ottawa, Ontario, Canada, June 16, 1994).

[3]*Cold Water,* prod. Noriko Ogami (Yarmouth, Maine: Intercultural Press, 1988), video cassette.

[4]Ibid.

[5]Denise Rotondo Fernandez, Dawn S. Carlson, Lee P. Stepina, and Joel D. Nicholson, "Hofested's Country Classification 25 Years Later," *Journal of Social Psychology* 137, no. 1 (1997): 43. The changing values are (1) the team approach, (2) a worldview shift from modern to postmodern and (3) more females in the workplace.

Chapter 5: Who's In Charge?

[1]Jaime S. Wurzel and Nancy K. Fischman, *A Different Place: The Intercultural Classroom* (Newtonville, Mass.: Intercultural Resource Corporation, 1994), pp. 27-30.

[2]Larke Nahme Huang and Sara Nieves-Grafals, "Cross-Cultural Counseling" (lecture given at the National Multicultural Institute, Washington, D.C., November 3-4, 1994).

[3]Ibid.

[4]Geert Hofested, *Culture's Consequences: International Differences in Work-Related Values* (Beverly Hills, Calif.: Sage, 1980), pp. 169-72.

[5]Ibid., p. 92.

Chapter 6: Who Am I?

[1]Jaime S. Wurzel and Nancy K. Fischman, *A Different Place: The Intercultural Classroom* (Newtonville, Mass.: Intercultural Resource Corporation, 1994), pp. 32-37.

[2]Ibid.

[3]Duane H. Elmer, *Cross-Cultural Conflict: Building Relationships for Effective Ministry* (Downers Grove, Ill.: InterVarsity Press, 1993), pp. 55-56.

[4]Richard Gesteland, "Successful Negotiations in Malaysia," *Worldwide Business Practices Report* 2, no. 12 (1995): 4.

Chapter 7: When Do We Start?

[1]Jaime S. Wurzel and Nancy K. Fischman, *A Different Place: The Intercultural Classroom* (Newtonville, Mass.: Intercultural Resource Corporation, 1994), p. 25.

[2]Ibid.

Chapter 8: What's Really Real?

[1]Darrell Whiteman, "Culture, Values, and Worldviews: Anthropology for Mission Practice" (lecture given at the Overseas Ministries Study Center in New Haven, Conn., January 1999).

[2]Some may add *antimodern*. Andrew Jones lectures worldwide on issues related to postmodernity.

[3]"Discerning the Times," *Leadership Network* 6 (Winter 2000): 1-4.

[4]Whiteman, "Culture, Values and Worldview" lecture.

[5]Ibid.

[6]Anne Fadiman, *The Spirit Catches You and You Fall Down* (New York: Noonday, 1997), p. 33.

[7]Steven C. Hawthorne, *Perspectives on the World Christian Movement Study Guide 1999 Edition* (Pasadena, Calif.: William Carey Library, 1999), p. 146.

[8]Fadiman, *Spirit Catches You*, p. 261.

[9]"The Temporary Gospel," *The Other Side* 11, no. 6 (1975):36-37. Permission granted.

Chapter 9: How Do You Resolve Conflict?

[1]David W. Augsburger, *Conflict Mediation Across Cultures* (Louisville, Ky.: Westminster John Knox, 1992), p. 5.

[2]Paul Pedersen, "Mediating Multicultural Conflict" (lecture given at the National Multicultural Institute in Washington, D.C., November 1994).

[3]Farid Elashmawi and Philip R. Harris, *Multicultural Management: New Skills for Global Success* (Houston, Tex.: Gulf Publishing Company, 1993), pp. 58, 61, 63.

[4]Duane Elmer, *Cross-Cultural Conflict: Building Relationships for Effective Ministry* (Downers Grove, Ill.: InterVarsity Press, 1993), p. 51.

[5]Augsburger, *Conflict Mediation*, p. 9.

[6]Ibid.

[7]Elmer, *Cross-Cultural Conflict*, pp. 67, 80, 99, 111.

[8]Gary Smalley and John Trent, *The Language of Love* (Pomona, Calif.: Focus on the Family, 1988), pp.16-17.

Chapter 10: God's Heart for Crosscultural Relationships

[1]Elie Wiesel, *From the Kingdom of Memory* (New York: Summit, 1990), p. 59.

[2]Robert McAfee Brown, *Unexpected News–Reading the Bible with Third World Eyes* (Philadelphia: Westminster Press, 1984), p. 19.

[3]Ibid., pp. 63-69.

[4]Elisabeth Farrell, "The World Is Coming to Us," *Charisma*, September 1996, p. 64.

[5]Oral presentation given at the Church in the 21st Century Conference in Phoenix, Ariz., June 25-28, 1995.

[6]Hazel Fellman, comp., *The Best Loved Poems of the American People* (Garden City, N.Y.: Garden City Books, 1936), pp.521-22, public domain.

[7]Farid Elashawi and Philip R. Harris, *Multicultural Management: New Skills for Global Success.* (Houston, Tex.: Gulf Publishing Company, 1993), pp. 58, 61, 63, permission granted.

Chapter 11: Putting It All Together

[1]Darrell Whiteman, "Culture, Values, and Worldviews: Anthropology for Mission

Practice" (lecture given at the Overseas Ministries Study Center in New Haven, Conn., January 1999).

[2]There are smaller breakdowns in these categories including Asian Indian, Chinese, Filipino, Japanese, Korean, Vietnamese, Guamanian or Chamorro, Samoan. U.S. Census Bureau, Census 2000.

Chapter 12: Just the Beginning
[1]Duane Elmer, *Cross-Cultural Conflict: Building Relationships for Effective Ministry* (Downers Grove, Ill.: InterVarsity Press, 1993), p. 13.

Appendix D: Preparing to Minister Within a Diverse Community
[1]Larke Nahme Huang and Sara Nieves-Grafals, "Cross-Cultural Counseling" (lecture given at the National Multicultural Institute, Washington, D.C., November 3-4, 1994).

Bibliography

Adeney, Bernard T. *Strange Virtues*. Downers Grove, Ill.: InterVarsity Press, 1995.

Augsburger, David. *Conflict Mediation Across Cultures*. Louisville, Ky.: Westminster John Knox, 1992.

Barger, Nancy, Tom Flautt and Helen Pelikan, facilitators. "Interplay of Culture and Type" (discussion at the conference for Successfully Applying the Myers-Briggs Type Indicator in Multicultural Settings; presented by the Pelikan Associates in Denver, Colo., April 27-29, 1992).

Brown, David McAffey. *Unexpected News—Reading the Bible with Third World Eyes*. Philadelphia, Penn.: Westminster Press, 1984.

Colson, Charles and Nancy Pearcey. *How Now Shall We Live?* Wheaton, Ill.: Tyndale House, 1999.

"Discerning the Times." *Next* 6 (Winter 2000).

Elashawi, Farid, and Philip R. Harris. *Multicultural Management New Skills for Global Success*. Houston, Tex.: Gulf Publishing Company, 1993.

Elmer, Duane H. *Cross-Cultural Conflict: Building Relationships for Effective Ministry*. Downers Grove, Ill.: InterVarsity Press, 1993.

Fadiman, Anne. *The Spirit Catches You and You Fall Down*. New York: Noonday Press, 1997.

Farrell, Elisabeth. "The World Is Coming to Us." *Charisma*, September 1996.

Fellman, Hazel, comp. *The Best Loved Poems of the American People*. Garden City, N.Y.: Garden City Books, 1936.

Fernandez, Denise Rotondo, Dawn S. Carlson, Lee P. Stepina and Joel D. Nicholson. "Hofested's Country Classifications 25 Years Later." *Journal of Social Psychology* 137, no. 1 (February 1997): 43.

Fuller, Graham E. *Secrets of Learning a Foreign Language*. Carlsbad, Calif.: Penton Overseas, 1992. Audio cassette.

Gamma Vision, Inc., "Culturally-Based Patterns of Difference." Kochman Communication Consultants, Ltd., San Francisco, Calif., 1989. Photocopied handout.

Gesteland, Richard. "Successful Negotiations in Malaysia." *Worldwide Business Practices* 2, no. 12 (1995): 4.

Hall, Edward T. *Beyond Culture*. Garden City, N.Y.: Anchor/Doubleday, 1976.

Hawthorne, Steven C. *Perspectives on the World Christian Movement Study Guide 1999 Edition*. Pasadena, Calif.: William Carey Library, 1999, p. 146.

Hofested, Geert. *Culture's Consequences: International Differences in Work-Related Values*. Beverly Hills, Calif.: Sage, 1980.

Huang, Larke Nahme and Sara Nieves-Grafals, "Cross-Cultural Counseling." Lecture given at the National Multicultural Institute, Washington, D.C., November 3-4, 1994.

Hughes, Robert. "The Fraying of America." *Time* 139, no. 5 (1992): 46-49.

Kohls, Robert L., and John M. Knight. *Developing Intercultural Awareness—A Cross-Cultural Training Handbook.* Yarmouth, Maine: Intercultural Press, 1994. Quoting John P. Fieg and John G. Blair. *There Is a Difference: Seventeen Intercultural Perspectives.* Washington: Meridian House International, 1975.

Martinez, Oscar J. *Border People: Life and Society in the U.S. Mexico Borderlands.* Tucson, Ariz.: University of Arizona Press, 1994.

Myers, Isabel Briggs, Mary H. McCaulley, Naomi L. Quenk and Allen L. Hammer. *MBTI Manual A Guide to the Development and Use of the Myers-Briggs Type Indicator,* Third Edition. Palo Alto, Calif.: Consulting Psychologists Press, 1998.

Ogami, Noriko, producer. *Cold Water.* Yarmouth, Maine: Intercultural Press, 1988. Video.

Pedersen, Paul and Allen Ivey. *Culture Centered Counseling and Interviewing Skills.* Westport, Conn.: Praeger, 1993.

Pedersen, Paul. "Mediating Multicultural Conflict." Lecture given at the National Multicultural Institute in Washington, D.C., November 1994.

Romo, Oscar. "Language Missions Leadership Conference." Lecture sponsored by Home Mission Board, Southern Baptist Convention, Los Angeles, Calif., February 23-26, 1990.

Singh, Robert. *The Farrakhan Phenomenon—Race, Reaction, and the Paranoid Style in American Politics.* Washington, D.C.: Georgetown University Press, 1997.

Smalley, Gary and John Trent. *The Language of Love.* Pomona, Calif.: Focus on the Family Publishing, 1988.

Storti, Craig. *Cross-Cultural Dialogues.* Yarmouth, Maine: Intercultural Press, 1994.

"The Temporary Gospel." *The Other Side.* November-December 1975: 36-37.

"Third Culture Kids," ed. Ruth Hill Useem (November 2001), TCK World <www.tckworld.com/useem/tckbibbook.html>.

Triandis, Harry C., Pierre K. Dasden and Alastair Heron. "Cross-Cultural Tests of Piaget's Theory." *The Handbook of Cross-Cultural Psychology.* Vol. 4, edited by William Wilson Lambert. Boston, Mass.: Allyn and Bacon, 1980.

U.S. Census Bureau. *American Demographics, U.S.A Today, Operation World, World Advance, Seattle Post Intelligence, Iranian Christians International.* Quoted in *Charisma,* October 1997.

Whiteman, Darrell. "Culture, Values, and Worldviews: Anthropology for Mission Practice." Lecture given at the Overseas Ministries Study Center in New Haven, Conn., 1999.

Wiesel, Elie. *From the Kingdom of Memory.* New York: Summit, 1990.

Wurzel, Jaime S., and Nancy K. Fischman. *A Different Place: The Intercultural Classroom.* Newtonville, Mass.: Intercultural Resource Corporation, 1994.

Zitek, Joanne and Cynthia Livingston. "Coaching and Giving Feedback in Multicultural Organizations." Paper presented at SIETAR International Congress, Ottawa, Ontario, Canada, June 16, 1994.

Suggested Reading

Axtell, Roger E., ed. *Do's and Taboos Around the World*. White Plains, N.Y.: John Wiley & Sons, 1993.

Bennett, Shane and Kim Felder. *Exploring the Land: Discovering Ways for Unreached People to Follow Christ*. Littleton, Colo.: Caleb Project, 1995.

Clay, Ele, ed. *Many Nations Under God*. Birmingham, Ala.: Women's Missionary Union, 1997.

————. *Project Help: Cultural Diversity Resource Kit*. Birmingham, Ala.: Women's Missionary Union, 1993.

Costa, Ruy O., ed. *One Faith, Many Cultures*. Maryknoll, N.Y.: Orbis, and Cambridge, Mass.: Boston Theological Institute, 1988.

Dunung, Sanjyot P. *Doing Business in Asia*. New York: Lexington Books, 1995.

Dyrness, William A., general ed. *Emerging Voices in Global Christian Theology*. Grand Rapids, Mich.: Zondervan, 1994.

Eddy, Robert. *Reflections on Multiculturalism*. Yarmouth, Maine: Intercultural Press, 1996.

Elmer, Duane H. *Cross-Cultural Conflict: Building Relationships for Effective Ministry*. Downers Grove, Ill.: InterVarsity Press, 1993.

Fong, Ken Uyeda. *Pursuing the Pearl: A Comprehensive Resource for Multi-Asian Ministry*. Valley Forge, Penn.: Judson Press, 1999.

Foster, Charles R. *Embracing Diversity*. Bethesda, Md.: The Alban Institute, 1997.

Gannon, Martin J. *Understanding Global Cultures*. Thousand Oaks, Calif.: Sage Publications, 1994.

Hassija, Jagdish and Mohini Panjabi, eds. *Visions of a Better World*. London: Brahma Kumaris World Spiritual University, 1993.

Halverson, Dean C., general ed. *The Compact Guide to World Religions*. Minneapolis, Minn.: Bethany House, 1996.

Hess, J. Daniel. *The Whole World Guide to Culture Learning*. Yarmouth, Maine: Intercultural Press, 1994.

Hesselgrave, David J. *Scripture and Strategy: The Use of the Bible in Postmodern Church and Mission*. Pasadena, Calif.: William Carey Library, 1994.

Hunsberger, George R., and Craig Van Gelder, eds. *The Church Between Gospel & Culture*. Grand Rapids, Mich.: Eerdmans, 1996.

Kohls, L. Robert and John M. Knight. *Developing Intercultural Awareness: A Cross-Cultural Training Handbook*. Yarmouth, Maine: Intercultural Press, 1994.

Landis, Dan, ed. *International Journal of Intercultural Relations*. Exeter, Great Britain: Elsevier Science Ltd., 1997.

Lee, Jung Lee. *The Trinity in Asian Perspective*. Nashville, Tenn.: Abingdon, 1996.

Lingenfelter, Sherwood G. *Agents of Transformation: A Guide for Effective Cross-Cultural Ministry*. Grand Rapids, Mich.: Baker, 1996.

Myers, Selma and Jonamay Lambert. *Managing Cultural Diversity*. Des Plaines, Ill.: Selma Myers and Jonamay Lambert, 1990.

———. *Beyond Awareness*. Des Plaines, Ill.: Selma Myers and Jonamay Lambert, 1992.

Ng, David, ed. *People on the Way*. Valley Forge, Penn.: Judson Press, 1996.

Ortiz, Manuel. *One New People: Models for Developing a Multiethnic Church*. Downers Grove, Ill.: InterVarsity Press, 1996.

Paniagua, Freddy A. *Assessing and Treating Culturally Diverse Clients*. Thousand Oaks, Calif.: Sage Publications, 1994.

Pedersen, Paul B. and Allen Ivey. *Culture-Centered Counseling and Interviewing Skills*. Westport, Conn.: Praeger Publishers, 1993.

Rhodes, Stephen A. *Where the Nations Meet: The Church in a Multicultural World*. Downers Grove, Ill.: InterVarsity Press, 1998.

Romano, Dugan. *Intercultural Marriage: Promise and Pitfalls*. Yarmouth, Maine: Intercultural Press, 1988.

Seelye, H. Ned, ed. *Experiential Activities for Intercultural Learning, Volume 1*. Yarmouth, Maine: Intercultural Press, 1996.

Simons, George F. and Amy Zuckerman. *Working Together: Succeeding in a Multi-Cultural Organization*. Menlo Park, Calif.: Crisp Publications, 1989, 1994.

Sire, James W. *The Universe Next Door*. Downers Grove, Ill.: InterVarsity Press, 1988.

Spencer, Aída Besançon and William David Spencer, eds. *The Global God– Multicultural Evangelical Views of God*. Grand Rapids, Mich.: Baker Books, 1998.

Stewart, Edward C. and Milton J. Bennett. *American Cultural Patterns: A Cross-Cultural Perspective*, rev. ed. Yarmouth, Maine: Intercultural Press, 1991.

Storti, Craig. *Cross-Cultural Dialogues*. Yarmouth, Maine: Intercultural Press, 1994.

———. *The Art of Crossing Cultures*. Yarmouth, Maine: Intercultural Press, 1990.

Wallis, Jim, ed. *Crossing the Racial Divide*. Washington, D.C.: Sojourners, 2000.

Wicks, Robert J. and Barry K. Estadt, eds. *Pastoral Counseling in a Global Church*. Maryknoll, N.Y.: Orbis, 1993.

Zahniser, A. H. Mathias. *Symbol and Ceremony: Making Disciples Across Cultures*. Monrovia, Calif.: Marc Publications, 1997.

J

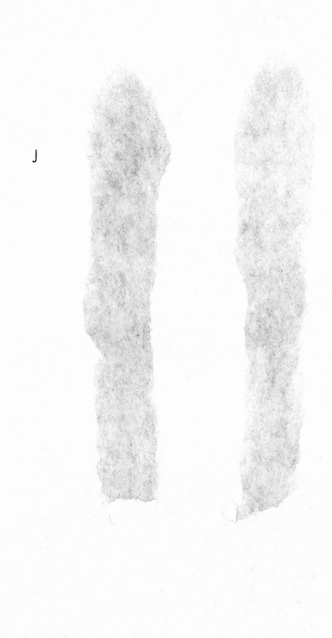